LIVING
JESUS

LIVING JESUS

Doing What Jesus Says in the Sermon on the Mount

Randy Harris
with Greg Taylor

LIVING JESUS
Doing What Jesus Says in the Sermon on the Mount

LEAFWOOD
PUBLISHERS
an imprint of Abilene Christian University Press

Copyright 2012 by Randy Harris

ISBN 978-089112-318-7

Printed in the United States of America

ALL RIGHTS RESERVED
No part of this publication may be reproduced, stored in a retrieval system, or transmitted in any form by any means—electronic, mechanical, photocopying, recording, or otherwise—without prior written consent.

Scripture quotations, unless otherwise noted, are from The Holy Bible, New International Version. Copyright 1984, International Bible Society. Used by permission of Zondervan Publishers.

Cover design by Marc Whitaker
Interior text design by Sandy Armstrong

Leafwood Publishers
1626 Campus Court
Abilene, Texas 79601
1-877-816-4455 toll free

For current information about all Leafwood titles, visit our Web site:
www.leafwoodpublishers.com

12 13 14 15 16 17 / 7 6 5 4 3 2 1

To the Allelon Community

They do what Jesus says

CONTENTS

Introduction	Doing What Jesus Says	9
Chapter 1	Start at the End: Wise and Foolish People	15
	Matthew 7:24–29	
Chapter 2	You Are Blessed	25
	Matthew 5:1–12	
Chapter 3	You Are Salt and Light	37
	Matthew 5:13–16	
Chapter 4	The Heart of the Law	45
	Matthew 5:17–20	
Chapter 5	Idiot! Stupid! Moron!	55
	Matthew 5:21–26	
Chapter 6	God Made Sex Really Good	65
	Matthew 5:27–32	
Chapter 7	Deep Integrity	75
	Matthew 5:33–37	
Chapter 8	Holy Prank!	85
	Matthew 5:38–48	
Chapter 9	Watch Me!	97
	Matthew 6:1–18	
Chapter 10	Treasures in Heaven	105
	Matthew 6:19–24	
Chapter 11	Stick in My Eye	115
	Matthew 7:1–14	
Chapter 12	Wolves in Sheep's Clothing	125
	Matthew 7:15–23	
	Living the Sermon	133
Further Reading		149

Introduction

DOING WHAT JESUS SAYS

For two thousand years many Christians have considered the Sermon on the Mount to be *the* most important words in the whole Bible. You would think that the words considered to be spoken by Jesus and written down would be easily interpreted and followed.

But over the centuries these words have become the most hotly debated words in history. And that's part of the problem. They've been debated more than followed. Some parts of the sermon are either so problematic or difficult that they've been left alone by preachers and teachers. Have you ever been invited by a church leader to shape your life around this teaching of Jesus? My guess is that you haven't.

This is your invitation to the most important teachings of Jesus Christ. There's a lot to know, but most importantly there's a lot to do. When it comes to the knowing part, I'm going to err on the side of non-technical explanations rather than complicated and detailed. Why? In order to focus on the doing of the words of Jesus.

Right here at the beginning I want to give you a brief sketch of how the Sermon on the Mount has been handled differently since Jesus' words were first written and passed down. Don't worry—I'm not going to bore you with a prolonged explanation of what scholars have said over two thousand years; but the broad strokes of the use of the Sermon on the Mount are fairly important to understand as we get started.

Early church leaders thought the words of Jesus could be practiced literally, and the *Didache*, a Christian document from the early second century, includes lots of language that sounds like words from the Sermon on the Mount.

In the fourth century when large numbers of people were baptized into the Catholic Church, Christian leaders began to make a distinction between those who *really* keep the hard teachings of Jesus (monks and bishops and the like) and those who are baptized adherents of the church who are expected to follow only the basic precepts.

So over the centuries, the Sermon on the Mount became something that was for extra credit. Eventually people believed the sermon was just too hard to do, that Jesus was proclaiming an ideal of the new kingdom, but that his words were not meant to be practiced literally. Some church leaders have even thought Jesus intentionally set a high standard to illustrate how far short we fall and how much we need the grace of God.

On the other hand, from the sixteenth century on, a group called the Anabaptists thought that Christians should practice the Sermon on the Mount literally, that there should be no difference between clergy (church leaders) and laity (regular folk) when it comes to following the words of Jesus.

In the last five hundred years the church has argued about whether Jesus really said everything in the sermon or whether Gospel writers just based it on true events of Jesus' oral teachings but bent it toward their own way of thinking. That would make the sermon a way of showing Christ's authority as the Messiah, rather than an actual manual for living.

The bottom line is that over two thousand years the church has believed and practiced the Sermon on the Mount in one or more of five ways:

1. We can do this.
2. Church leaders can do this but it's too hard for regular folk.
3. These teachings of Christ are too hard for anyone, and if we try to follow them it leads to legalism.
4. The teachings are too hard but they show our need for God's grace; keeping the laws literally is not the point.
5. Yes, they are too hard but by God's blessing and grace we must try to keep them.

My journey has taken me through all of these approaches as I've studied, heard, prayed, and tried to live the sermon. But I have come closer to the fifth category than ever before. This book is the story of how I've gotten there and what I'm trying to do about it. And it's an invitation to you to come with me, to live the sermon, to do what Jesus says. Category number five above is really a return to what the early church thought: We can do this. But we certainly need God's empowerment and grace in order to obey what Jesus says.

So this book is not just a study of the Sermon on the Mount. It's a way of discovering what Jesus says so we can do what Jesus says. My intention is not to add information or advance scholarship about the Sermon on the Mount. The simple historical sketch I just gave is about as much as we need for our purposes.

What I've written here is different from other writings on the Sermon on the Mount. For more than two thousand years we have benefited from scholars, translators, and interpreters who have indeed debated and taken different positions on the words of Christ, yet they have been talking about the most important words we have on record of the teachings of Jesus. I believe that by using the best translations available and accepting that these words were written based on the oral teachings of Christ and written down for us by Matthew and Luke, we must take these words seriously as a rule of life. In fact, many Christian communities throughout the centuries have based their rules of living together on the words of this sermon.

So I'm not attempting to write a scholarly book on the Sermon on the Mount. I'm trying to provide a field manual for living the life Jesus wants for us.

This book, which includes content from a film series I did by the same name, can stand alone, or it can be used along with the DVD as a field manual for groups or individuals who want, not only to know more about the Sermon on the Mount, but also to live what it teaches.

The Sermon on the Mount is full of hard teachings, but at my core I believe Jesus wants us to live out these teachings, however imperfectly. I believe also that by living these teachings Jesus gives us incredible and abundant life. He even promises that if we practice the commands and teach others to do so, we will be called "great in the kingdom of heaven." He says that those who hear his words and put them into practice are wise. Those who do not are foolish.

Jesus didn't intentionally make this so hard we can't possibly live any of these teachings. I believe the teachings are doable, but the problem is that the church has long taught that these truths are so unattainable and impractical that they've simply been ignored.

What G. K. Chesterton said about the Christian life is particularly true about the Sermon on the Mount: "The Christian ideal has not been tried and found wanting; it has been found difficult and left untried."

Not only has it been found difficult and left untried, but even to suggest following the Sermon on the Mount as literally as possible—we'll make plucking out your eyes and cutting off your hands a quick exception—appears to many as some sort of fanaticism.

I teach at a small university in Texas. Each year I stand in front of eager—and sometimes not so eager—students and teach them the truths in the Sermon on the Mount. I always have to convince them that Jesus is really serious about living this life. This isn't "Suggestions on the Mount." This isn't Jesus raising the bar so high that we can only try and fail and so learn a lesson about the grace of God—though certainly that will happen over and over in our lives.

No, this is Jesus standing in the hills around Capernaum, probably overlooking the Sea of Galilee, a breeze blowing, and eager—and some not so eager—people hanging on Jesus' words. Some wanted to catch him in theological corners and then try to paint him in. Others wanted just to be healed of diseases. Still others heard those words and believed that they could follow Jesus and do what he said.

So, here is the beginning and the end of the Sermon on the Mount: doing what Jesus says. And that's what this book is about.

The question for us is not, "Can you do these teachings?" They are doable but not doable perfectly, so expect some failure, some resistance from yourself and others.

No, the question is, "Will you try?" This book is a field guide for those who choose to try.

Chapter One

START AT THE END: WISE AND FOOLISH PEOPLE
Matthew 7:24-29

Therefore everyone who hears these words of mine and puts them into practice is like a wise man who built his house on the rock. The rain came down, the streams rose, and the winds blew and beat against that house; yet it did not fall, because it had its foundation on the rock. But everyone who hears these words of mine and does not put them into practice is like a foolish man who built his house on sand. The rain came down, the streams rose, and the winds blew and beat against that house, and it fell with a great crash.

When Jesus had finished saying these things, the crowds were amazed at his teaching, because he taught as one who had authority, and not as their teachers of the law.

I've known people who start a book at the back to find out how it ends. I've seen people read magazines backwards. Quirky. Sorry, maybe you are one of them? Why do you do this? You must have a reason.

Or there are those people who must begin a conversation or meeting by saying, "Okay, here's the goal of our meeting today . . . ." They begin at the end.

But for the rest of us who believe basically that stories and sermons have beginnings, middles, and endings, we scratch our heads when someone starts in a weird spot. The beginning is called that for a reason!

So if you have ever read the Sermon on the Mount and you know that it starts in Matthew 5 and ends in Matthew 7, then you might be wondering why I'm starting this book on the Sermon on the Mount with the very last section of Jesus' teaching. Why start at the end? Good question. Because this ending impacts the way we read the rest of the sermon. At least, for me, the foundation of the sermon is found at the end, and I'd like to convince you of that too.

To illustrate this for one of my freshman Bible classes, we met in the beautiful Chapel on the Hill on the Abilene Christian University campus. The chapel is one of the places where we come to worship together; the sound of young and passionate voices singing praises reverberates off the high ceilings and walls and stirs my heart.

It stirs my heart when I stand in front of these students and think of how they want to change the world. It puts urgency in my heart that they need a foundation in the teachings of Jesus in order to form their own lives before they ever can change the world.

This urgency has led me on a profound journey to discover the best way to shape young hearts and minds in the way of Jesus. I began more than a decade ago trying to learn everything I possibly could about how to give college students an experience that they'll never forget the rest of their lives.

These four years of college will be a whirlwind for them, and then they'll be out in the world building their careers, families, and homes. They'll have a literal place to live but figuratively they'll build a house and, depending on the foundation they build on, the house will either stand like Gibraltar or crash like the stock market of 1929.

So I take my freshmen to the words of Jesus and point them to a pursuit that is more than academic: it's a life. Jesus said that if you hear these words of mine and put them into practice, you are like a wise man who built his house on a concrete slab. When the storms that will surely come for all these students blow their doors down and they are soaking wet and worn out, their house will not crash because they have put their faith in Jesus by putting his words into practice.

I think of the Chapel on the Hill and my freshmen Bible students because of the way I believe the Sermon on the Mount ought to be introduced. I believe the foundation of the sermon is found at the end. And so these young people come to this hill that is built on a strong foundation and we get a sense of the image Jesus was painting at the end of the sermon that actually makes a great introduction for understanding the whole thing.

The end of the sermon provides a clue to the question that determines how you read the whole sermon. The question is this: Can you do this?

Can you really live this way?

Does Jesus actually intend for you to shape your life around the Sermon on the Mount? Or has Jesus intentionally set an ideal so high that you can't possibly live up to it? Is the purpose of the Sermon on the Mount to convince you that you're a bad person? Is the purpose to convince you that, even when you've done your best, you've still not measured up, that you really are a bad person, and there's nothing you can do but simply fall on the grace of God?

Can you do this?

If you've come to the conclusion that Jesus really intends for you to live this way, and you can, then the sermon becomes the guide to practical living. It's what shapes your day-to-day life. If you decide you can't, it's a lot of beautiful theory but may not have anything to do with how you go out and live life tomorrow. So my question to you is this: Can you do this? Do you really believe that Jesus intends for us to live this way?

I am a frustrated intermediate chess player. I learned to play chess from a student years ago when I taught at Lipscomb University. He was a flaky student and had all sorts of problems. He liked to play chess and I thought, *This is a really good idea.* I'll be able to spend a lot of time with him because the only thing I knew about chess was that it was a really slow game. So he taught me how to play chess, and I discovered that I actually love the game. It is a wonderful game, but it's also extremely frustrating. There is nothing more frustrating than losing a chess game. In other games, like cards or baseball, you can always blame a loss on the deal or a bad bounce, but when you get beat in chess, the reason is this: you're stupid.

There is absolutely no luck in chess. You've got to take total responsibility for your losses. And so this student knew how to play. I didn't. He was winning all the time. It was extremely frustrating to me because he was basically a C+ student. So I decided that I was going to get sneaky and learn to play better. To learn to play chess better in a sneaky way, you do one of two things: you either play computer chess or you go read a book. I started doing both. So I go to the bookstore, and I want to buy a chess book, and it's so intimidating when you're a beginning chess player. There are rows and rows of chess books. How can you pick one out of all these books?

So I picked the one that said, *How to Play Winning Chess.* I picked this one because that seems to be to the point. So I bought the book and began reading about all the major moves. The first major chapter was on Checkmate. And I thought, *Well, this doesn't make any sense.* The book is teaching me how to checkmate, and I'll never get a chance to checkmate. You know, by the time you get around to checkmate all my pieces are gone. But the author of the chess book says you should be thinking about the goal of the game from the very first move. You think about the game with reference to the end.

So I'm doing something a little unusual in my teaching of the Sermon on the Mount. The first text I want us to consider is the last text in the sermon. I begin with the last text because how we read that last text determines how we read the whole sermon.

After Jesus lays out all this profound teaching, he closes the sermon with a Vacation Bible School song: "The Wise Man Built His House on the Rock." Many of my freshmen Bible class students remember Vacation Bible School fondly, and maybe you do, too. The stuff of Vacation Bible School memories is made of grape Kool-Aid, lots of cookies, flannelgraph stories, and songs with hand motions like "The Wise Man." The song goes:

> The wise man built his house upon the rock.
> The wise man built his house upon the rock.
> The wise man built his house upon the rock,
> And the house on the rock stood firm.
>
> The foolish man built his house on the sand.
> The foolish man built his house on the sand.
> The foolish man built his house on the sand
> And the house on the sand went smash!

Here is where the kids love to clap their hands and yell, "Smash!"

Jesus says the wise person is the one who hears these sayings and puts them into practice. And the foolish person is the one who hears these sayings and doesn't put them into practice. And this is stunning because at the end of the sermon Jesus places no emphasis on *understanding* and all the emphasis on *doing*.

The sermon is not a body of material to be cognitively mastered. It's a life to be lived. And here we come to a fork in the road. Nearly everybody knows Martin Luther and his wonderful, powerful explication of the grace of God. When Luther looked at the Sermon on the Mount, he basically said, "Look, nobody can do this. The bar's too high. The standards are impossible. Nobody can do this. What this sermon is really about is pointing out to you that you are unable to be righteous, so that what you will do is throw yourself upon the grace of God when you discover you can't really do this."

Well, Luther's take on the Sermon on the Mount is a profound thought. There's just one problem with it. Jesus doesn't agree with it.

What Jesus says, instead, is that the wise person is the one who hears these sayings and puts them into practice. So we have to decide from the beginning how we're going to read this sermon. And this is the way I'm going to read it. It is the most practical, realistic way to live the Christian life that you can imagine. It's not some impossibly high ideal set in the heavens to make you feel bad because you can't live up to it. Jesus actually expects us to do this stuff. He thinks you can live out your life in this sort of way.

So we all have a decision to make in the very beginning.

If you look at the sermon and say, "Oh, those are really good ideas, but we can't really do it," then you only get one view of the sermon, one truth about grace that Luther points out. It's a profound thought about God's grace, but it's not what Jesus intended.

But if you look at the sermon and say, "This is the way life is as Jesus intended it, and he actually calls us to live this life," then you read the sermon in a completely different way.

Let's go back to the chess game. Remember that the chess book said to keep the goal in mind—the checkmate? Before we go back to the beginning of the sermon, we need to look at the end. Do you really think that this is a life that can be lived? More specifically, do you think Jesus is talking about a life that you can live?

One of my favorite half-true stories is about the guy in Los Angeles who got bored. And when you're bored you have to do something, and so he attached dozens of helium balloons to his lawn chair. He had it all weighted down. Then he got himself a BB gun and a sack full of PBJs—that's not ammo, that's peanut butter and jelly sandwiches. He figured he was going to float up for a couple hundred feet. Then he would look around a while, eat a PBJ or two, and when he got bored again—bored of flying!—he'd use his BB gun and shoot balloon by balloon until he simply floated gently back to earth. Great plan.

Now anybody should see that there are all sorts of problems with this plan. He didn't. Unfortunately he was not an engineer, and he didn't know that he had too much balloon for himself. And so when he cuts his rope he doesn't go up a couple hundred feet. He goes up a couple thousand feet. And he drifts into the landing pattern of LAX airport. Can you imagine being on a plane, looking out your window, and seeing a guy in a lawn chair eating a peanut butter sandwich with a BB gun across his lap?

And so he starts shooting his balloons. It takes him hours and hours to get down because he's drifted so high that, by the time he gets down, every reporter in Los Angeles is there, and they all have the same question for him: *How could you do something so stupid?*

And the lawn chair balloon guy's answer was priceless. He said, "Well, you can't just sit around. You got to do something."

That's Jesus' guy. You can't only sit around studying this stuff. You can't just sit around thinking how profound it is. At some point you've got to do something. And the good news is, Jesus says you can. This is not only a life that should be lived. It's a life that *can* be lived. At least that's Jesus' opinion.

At the conclusion, Jesus says, "The wise person is the one who hears these sayings of mine and puts them into practice." So I want to ask you again: Can you do this?

The most devastatingly bad misreading of the sermon is to think that this is a life no one can live. Jesus is trying in this sermon to be as practical and as realistic as he can about how life ought to be lived. He's not trying to intimidate you. He's not trying to put you down. He's not trying to say, "Okay, let me set this ideal for you and then you'll see what bad people you really are." No, he's calling you into a way of life that can be lived and we generally haven't read the sermon that way.

We read the sections of the sermon and say, "Oh boy, I don't think I could ever do that." And Jesus says, "Wisdom is found in hearing this and doing it, and foolishness is found in hearing this and not doing it."

This sermon is not simply meant to be understood. This sermon is to be lived. It's to be practiced. So now this is where I ask the question and answer it.

Can you?

Absolutely!

The Jesus who *calls* you to live this way is the Jesus who *empowers* you to live this way. Can you?

Discussing What Jesus Says
Read Matthew 7:24-29

The Sermon on the Mount is the most practical, realistic way to live the Christian life that you can imagine. Jesus actually expects us to do this stuff. He thinks you can live out your life in this sort of way. Now, it's up to you as you read: "Will you?"

How does the image of the wise man and the foolish man illustrate the way we keep the teachings of the Sermon on the Mount?

Do you think the Sermon on the Mount is doable?

Is the Sermon on the Mount so hard that all you can do is know you are a failure and fall on God's grace?

Is this life Jesus is describing one you think you can live?

The first question is, *Can you?* And if you answer yes to that question, the next question is, *Will you?*

Doing What Jesus Says

After each chapter is a challenge to do what Jesus says in the Sermon on the Mount. This first challenge is simple yet the most profound and important step you will take, so it is not to be taken lightly.

Spend a week or more asking yourself one question: "Am I willing to do what Jesus says?"

The question is not only, "Can I?" The question is ultimately, *Will I do what Jesus says?*

If Jesus tells you that you can, then it's not a question of ability. It's only a question of will. That's why we start at the end of the sermon rather than the beginning.

So, as we look at the rest of the sermon together, we have to keep this in mind. Jesus intends for us to live this way, and we can. That's the single most important interpretive move in hearing the sermon. It's practical advice on how to live the life in Jesus.

Now, it's up to you as you read. This week ask yourself, Will I?

Chapter Two

YOU ARE
BLESSED
Matthew 5:1–12

Now when Jesus saw the crowds, he went up on a mountainside and sat down. His disciples came to him, and he began to teach them.
He said:
    Blessed are the poor in spirit,
        for theirs is the kingdom of heaven.
Blessed are those who mourn,
        for they will be comforted.
Blessed are the meek,
        for they will inherit the earth.
Blessed are those who hunger and thirst for righteousness,
        for they will be filled.
Blessed are the merciful,
        for they will be shown mercy.

Blessed are the pure in heart,
 for they will see God.
Blessed are the peacemakers,
 for they will be called children of God.
Blessed are those who are persecuted because of righteousness,
 for theirs is the kingdom of heaven.
 Blessed are you when people insult you, persecute you and falsely say all kinds of evil against you because of me. Rejoice and be glad, because great is your reward in heaven, for in the same way they persecuted the prophets who were before you.

As we saw in the previous chapter, it's best to start at the end of the Sermon on the Mount because in the ending Jesus squarely places the emphasis on doing his teachings and not merely understanding them—and certainly not ignoring them or running scared from them. So this impacts how we read the rest of the sermon with the emphasis on doing. We need this foundation that comes from hearing and doing the words of Jesus. But we can't do anything without the very beginning of the sermon either.

Jesus begins the Sermon on the Mount with blessings, and he blesses the people who are most desperate for them: the poor, the humble, those who are persecuted, those who mourn.

This is one of the things I love best about the Sermon on the Mount: Jesus knows that we can't follow him until we know his blessing.

I'm convinced the world needs the blessing of God in order to practice the words of the Sermon on the Mount. I'm not talking about the now ubiquitous Christian leave-taking quickie blessing, "Have a blessed day." I'm talking about truly living under the powerful blessing of God even in those times when you think you are anything but blessed.

These sayings are often called Beatitudes, and though it's similar to the word attitude, it really comes from a Latin word that means happy. Beatitude is not a word that refers to attitude, though some confuse Jesus' blessings with a list of positive mental attitude steps. A positive attitude is something good to have, but that's not what Jesus is talking about here.

There's a gravestone at Buffalo Gap Cemetery in West Texas that belongs to a little girl named Sally. She was born in 1892 and died in 1899 at the age of seven. They've been burying people like Sally and families have been coming to this cemetery to mourn for more than a hundred years. If you listen carefully you can still almost hear them.

My best friend in high school committed suicide. And I wonder if the people at my friend's funeral could believe that those who mourn are blessed. I've presided over dozens of funerals at places like Buffalo Gap Cemetery, and I've prayed that prayer that God will bless those who are standing about. Sometimes it's hard to believe it when Jesus says that places of mourning can be places of blessing.

It's interesting that when Jesus starts out the Sermon on the Mount, he doesn't begin with commands. I want us to understand why that's the order he chose.

Can we really believe this? Can we really believe that in the most difficult times in our lives God is going to be there with blessing?

When Jesus started to teach the crowds, the first words out of his mouth were these: "blessed are. . . ." It's funny how we really haven't paid very much attention to the first word because we have tended to read these first words of Jesus as commands rather than blessings. We're saying you better be poor in spirit. We're treating the beginning of the sermon as commands: you better be pure in heart! You better mourn!

But Jesus is not giving commands here. As we'll see later in the sermon, he gives plenty of commands. But that's not the first thing out of his mouth. Instead, the first thing he does is offer blessings to the people who are there. I think the first words in the sermon are absolutely beautiful: *Blessed are the poor in spirit.*

Poor in spirit is a loaded term. It refers back to a Hebrew word: the *anawim*. And if you understand who the *anawim* are, you hear the power of these words. One of the most powerful ways to understand *anawim* is to remember that the nation of Israel was hauled into exile, but not everybody was taken into exile. The enemies of Israel actually took into exile only those people who were useful. If you weren't useful at all, you got left behind. Now, you haven't really been insulted until the enemy says, "We're going to haul off everybody who is useful, but we're not going to take you." And there was a word for those people. They were the *anawim*. The pathetic. The pitiful. The worthless.

And this is really important because most of us are going to have some *anawim* moments in our lives. We all like to think of ourselves as winners, but we're basically not. We're basically mostly losers and we spend most of our time losing and then there are those times when we have the really spectacular losses.

I remember my first experience of *anawim*—it was on my intramural softball team at Harding University. They would put at least twelve people on every team because you play with ten, and there's always a couple of people who can't be there and if everybody happened to show up you'd have to take turns sitting on the bench. Well, on this particular night I'm sitting on the bench and I look out in the field and I see that my team only has nine players out there. And I'm sitting on the bench. You haven't been properly insulted until your team says, "We would prefer to play shorthanded than have you out here with us. We'd prefer to have you on the bench." That was an *anawim* moment in my life.

My next big *anawim* moment was when I applied for a job at a school. I was right out of graduate school and they didn't hire me. Now, that doesn't make me *anawim*. What does make me *anawim* is this: they hired nobody. Now think about it. It's one thing to apply for a job and finish second to a really good candidate. I applied for a job and finished second to nobody. They said, "We've thought it over and we think we would rather have nobody than have you." *Anawim*.

What about you? Do you recall your *anawim* moments? They are more than embarrassing moments we share at the party. These are those times when you truly feel rejected, and you wonder how you could ever recover. You feel hopeless and alone.

We all have *anawim* moments. Even those voted "Most Likely to Succeed" in high school have their *anawim* moments. These overachievers may feel rejection by parents unless they turn in flawless report cards and extracurricular achievements are nothing short of scholarship-worthy. *Anawim*. Those who have felt the sting of a spouse's unfaithfulness know what it's like to be one of the *anawim*.

In nearly every culture and time, the poor know what it's like to be *anawim*. Even people in churches who don't immediately display some outward gifts or assets that a church can use know what it's like to be rejected as *anawim*.

That crowd that showed up out there on that mountain to hear the Sermon on Mount was the *anawim*, and the first words out of Jesus' mouth were these: Blessed are the *anawim* for theirs is the kingdom of heaven.

I want you to imagine what you would have thought if you had heard those words. For all your life you'd been told that you're too pathetic, you're too pitiful, you're too worthless for God's love, and the first words out of Jesus' mouth is to affirm God's love for you.

Blessed are the *anawim*. For those who face rejection over and over, you are blessed as important in the kingdom of God.

Blessed are those who mourn. For those who mourn for a little girl buried in the Buffalo Gap Cemetery or for my best friend who committed suicide, you are blessed with comfort from the Almighty God who knows of your great loss.

Blessed are the meek. For it doesn't look like you must have a large ego to be noticed by God. So for those who put more stock in God than in themselves, they will inherit the earth.

Blessed are those who hunger and thirst for righteousness. For they will be filled with what they are looking for.

Blessed are the merciful, for they will be shown mercy.

And then he says, "Blessed are the pure of heart," and that's not so much about moral purity as it is about having singleness of purpose in life. He says that's a blessed way to live. And what's really interesting about this whole section is not the individual words; it's when you take them all together and see that

Jesus' idea of the blessed life and our idea of the blessed life have almost nothing in common.

Blessed are the peacemakers, for they will be called children of God. Have you ever noticed that nobody really appreciates a peacemaker? You know, those people who refuse to get drawn into the violence and confusion and hostility of their age, but simply by their presence create peace—and Jesus says they are blessed and that this is to be our way of life.

Blessed are those who are persecuted because of righteousness, for theirs is the kingdom of heaven. Jesus says it's even possible for you to have a blessed life, a good life, when you're persecuted because God's got you. Even, as he says, "when people insult you, persecute you and falsely say all kinds of evil against you because of me, you are blessed."

So what is Jesus really trying to accomplish here by blessing the *anawim*, the mourners, the peacemakers, the persecuted? What's he driving at? Can we really make ourselves meeker or look for opportunities to be persecuted?

Well, certainly we could practice a lifestyle that leads to humility (see "Doing What Jesus Says" at the end of this chapter for challenges on humility), or we can obey the teachings of Christ so radically that it subjects us to persecution, but here's another way of translating what Jesus is doing. He's saying, "Okay, let me describe to you what the good life really is."

In American culture, in contrast, we've been told that the good life is having all the stuff you want. The good life is having the perfect family. The good life is being able to retire early. The good life is having total security. Then Jesus comes along and says, "No, the blessed life is knowing that God loves you and you're in God's hands."

I think it is impossible to live out the commands of the Sermon on the Mount without first receiving this blessing. If you try to live out the commands of the Sermon on the Mount without being blessed by God, without feeling loved by God, without knowing that God is holding you close to his side, you're going to grind away and you're never going to get there.

Why? Because if that's the approach you take, you are attempting to win God's favor by keeping a set of arbitrary commands. You're trying to make yourself loved rather than doing it out of response to the love that God's already given. Don't think it's any accident that Jesus doesn't start with commands. He starts with blessings. And my question is this: Do you feel blessed by God?

I'm convinced that most of our world feels as if it's under a curse. What would it be like to live in a world where people know they are truly loved and blessed by God? Because there are going to be a lot more *anawim* in the world than there will ever be winners. We're told there's room at the top, but there's not much.

Only a couple of people can be at the top and everyone else is going to be *anawim*. And in a world like that, it's really important to know that the poor in spirit are God's dearly beloved people. When we receive that blessing, then we're empowered to live out the commands.

When I first started studying the Sermon on the Mount, I thought the Beattitudes were orders to be obeyed rather than blessings to be enjoyed. One of the things I've discovered in my years of teaching is how desperate students are for a word of blessing.

Everybody tells them what they do wrong or get wrong, but it really makes a big difference when they feel as if they're blessed. When those people came out to that mountain to see Jesus, nobody brought a pencil, nobody brought a notebook, and they weren't there for a seminar. They were out there looking for life and the first word out of Jesus' mouth to those people is this: You are blessed.

The people on the mountain that day were occupied by a foreign country. Many of them were poor. They were the marginalized people of society. And Jesus wanted them to know from the very beginning that God loved them, and they were blessed by God because the rest of the world told them that they were throw away people, *anawim*.

And what about us? Don't we need a blessing, too? There's a world out there telling us we're not good enough. Those people came to that mountain needing a blessing. And we come to this teaching of Jesus needing a blessing, too.

There are a lot of commands in the Sermon on the Mount, and through the rest of this series we'll look at those commands; but I believe it's impossible to live out the Sermon on the Mount if we don't first understand that we are loved and blessed by God. We all pursue the American dream. We all want what is described as the good life, but Jesus reassures us that the good life is found in unexpected places. Places like Buffalo Gap Cemetery. Places of mourning. The good life, counter-intuitively, is found in places of persecution and even in places of poverty. The good life can be found in these places, too, because God's love is what produces good life.

The Sermon on the Mount begins with blessings, not commands—blessings for people who usually aren't. What about you? Do you believe you're blessed by God? There are a lot more losers in the world than there are winners. There are a lot more people who are poor and on the outside of society than those who are at the top. And Jesus words come ringing down through the years.

Regardless of what your world says, this is the truth of the matter: In God's eyes you are blessed.

Discussing What Jesus Says
Read Matthew 5:1–12

Jesus begins the Sermon on the Mount not with commands or difficult mysteries but with a word of blessing for the humble in heart.

Do you tend to read these statements of Jesus as commands or blessings?

Can we really believe that in most difficult times in our lives God is going to be there with blessing?

Do you believe you are now living with or without the blessing of God?

Do you feel blessed by God?

Do you believe that God blesses the poor? Do you believe God blesses people who mourn? Those who suffer persecution?

Doing What Jesus Says

In order to cultivate the life of meekness or humility, here are some exercises to practice over a period of one to two weeks:

Speech: When someone compliments you, respond with a simple "Thank you."

When you fail, give no excuses. Simply say, "I'm sorry."

In every interaction with others, take a posture of listening rather than talking.

Dress: Do not wear clothing that leads to pride or self-consciousness.

Work: Do "dirty jobs" like washing dishes or pulling weeds or serving someone alone and in secret if at all possible.

Read Philippians 2. The humility of Jesus is at the heart of the Sermon on the Mount.

Remember, the goal is not to think less of ourselves but to think of ourselves less.

Chapter Three

YOU ARE SALT AND LIGHT
Matthew 5:13–16

You are the salt of the earth. But if the salt loses its saltiness, how can it be made salty again? It is no longer good for anything, except to be thrown out and trampled underfoot.

You are the light of the world. A town built on a hill cannot be hidden. Neither do people light a lamp and put it under a bowl. Instead they put it on its stand, and it gives light to everyone in the house. In the same way, let your light shine before others, that they may see your good deeds and glorify your Father in heaven.

Early on in the sermon Jesus uses images of salt and light to talk about Christians interacting with the world. Jesus' images of salt and light have become part of the Christian vocabulary. In fact, every Christian worth his or her, uh, salt wants to be salt and light. We often say, "She is salt of the earth in her neighborhood" or "He really shines his light where he works." Still I wonder, do we really have a very good operational definition of what Jesus meant by salt and light, and if so, do we have the courage to start leaning into that definition and living that way? So in this chapter I want us to discover or re-discover what it really means to be a city set on the hill or to be salt that changes the nature of the world.

I find it interesting that both salt and light require two things. First, the elements salt and light need to be different from the things that they are a part of. Light seems to be most useful where there is darkness. Salt is most useful added to bland food. Second, salt and light need to penetrate their environment or other ingredients in order to make a difference in them.

I meet regularly in my living room with a group of honors ministry students who intend to make a difference in the world. They are idealistic, sharp-witted, good-hearted, and energetic, and so I regularly ask them questions we can discuss, and we learn from one another as we think about the words of Jesus.

One day I asked the group that had gathered, "Is there too much world in the church or is there too little church in the world?" They received the question much like many others I had posed: with thoughtfulness and creativity.

Using Jesus' images of salt and light, we discussed what it means to be different from our surroundings and what it means to penetrate our surroundings. So the question phrased another way is this: Are Christians so separate from the world that they can't make any difference in the world? Or have Christians become so much like the world that they're not different enough to make any difference?

"Christians don't stand out enough for people to ask, 'What makes you different?' And this gives us the chance to talk about the difference Jesus makes in our lives," one student said.

Another student said the church is split racially and by generations much like the rest of the world. The quote most often attributed to Martin Luther King, Jr. remains true in the twenty-first century: "Sunday morning is the most segregated time in America."

Students lamented that churches are less welcoming than condemning and judging. People don't feel as if they are part of a church body at all.

On the other hand, students critiqued the church as often watering down the gospel so much that the church doesn't look anything like Jesus. Why? Because we want people to come to church and not feel discomfort. So we change the gospel to make it easier to swallow.

One student said, "I don't think that there's anything that distinguishes us. It seems like Christianity has become like just another check box. Are you Republican, Democrat, Christian, Muslim? Check the appropriate box. Christianity is more a radical way of changing the way that you look at everything else. It's not a subdivision; it's a way of life that changes the way you look at everything else." Other students agreed. One said, "Christianity has become a demographic."

Another student said Christianity today has become prefab, so that Christians seem to attempt to live up to what has already been defined as light and salt, but the heart is not there.

Finally, a student concluded the discussion this way: "One thing I've noticed is that if you really are going to start living this way and you start making big changes in your life, eventually it starts to change who you are from the inside out. The more you live the teachings out, the more it becomes natural to you—it's who you are. And once you get there, you end up living a life that creates peace among everyone you are around."

These students understand that the Sermon on the Mount is calling Christians to a way of life, not a demographic choice like checking a box. So what does it look like when we live out this passage, when we're salt and light in the world? What do you think that looks like?

We are followers of Jesus, not just for ourselves but for the sake of the world, and the Sermon on the Mount is a call to Christians to live for the sake of the world. The world needs light. The world needs salt. It doesn't need a bunch of Christians crawling into their Christian storm shelter and never coming out because it's not safe out there, nor do we need a bunch of Christians who look so much like the world that they can't see the light. They can't see the city set on the hill. Jesus calls us to follow him for the sake of the world. We are the light of the world. We are the salt of the earth. If that's who we are, it's time we start to look like that.

Maybe some of these words in the Sermon on the Mount are familiar to you. If you are like me, when you come to familiar words like this, you let your eyes pass right over them and you don't really let the words sink in and register and connect with how you are living your life. We say, "Yeah, yeah, yeah, okay, what else?"

In Jesus' time a lamp on a stand was all the light you had. Salt was used as currency. These were fairly important elements of life. So I think we ought not yada, yada our way through parts of his teaching. So read through these words again, slowly.

You are the salt of the earth, but if salt loses its saltiness it's then good for nothing except to be thrown out and trampled by men. It can't be made salty again. You're the light of the world. A city set on a hill cannot be hidden; neither do men light a lamp and put it under a bowl, but instead they put it on a lamp stand so it gives light to all that are in the house. Let your light so shine before men that they may see your good works and glorify your father in Heaven.

This is strange language. He's not saying you ought to be salt. He's not saying you ought to be light. Jesus is saying you *are* salt. Jesus is saying you *are* light. You are.

This reminds me of one of the more favorite things I get to do as a preacher. I occasionally get asked to preach weddings. I don't really like to do weddings, but there's that one moment in the wedding I really like, and that's where I get to create something new by simply saying the words, "I now pronounce you husband and wife." And the moment before I say this, they weren't husband and wife. But when I say "you are," they become husband and wife. It is a feeling of incredible power—of course I'm being facetious, but it does keep me interested in a task I would otherwise not want to do.

I remember one time when I married a couple who were already married, and I didn't get the same thrill out of it. I was getting ready to do the ceremony for this young couple, and I asked the guy, "Where's the wedding license?"

He replies, "There isn't one. I need to talk to you."

And I got worried. I thought, *Oh brother he's got some wife in Kansas or something,* and so we go to a back room and he says, "We couldn't wait to get married. We eloped a week ago."

"Oh."

He asks me if that's okay.

"It's great," I said, "We can't mess this up. How many people here know that?"

"Nobody knows," he said.

So I did the wedding. I married them. I said the fateful words, "I now pronounce you husband and wife," but there was no power in them.

So to keep it interesting, I quickly flipped off my microphone and said, "I now pronounce you husband and wife . . . still."

And they laughed so hard they couldn't kiss and everybody at the reception afterwards was asking them, "What did he say to you?"

Those words just didn't have the same power because I didn't create the reality. Those of you who are married know this: Once I pronounce them husband and wife, at least the guy is going to spend the rest of his life trying to become what I just told him he was because he knows nothing about being a husband. I pronounce him husband and then he spends the rest of his life trying to become a husband.

It's the same way in these words, "You are . . . salt and light."

You hear this strange language in this text. You are. Jesus doesn't say you ought to be salt, you ought to be light. He tells us, "You are." You are the salt of the earth. You are the light of the world. And then what we have to do is spend the rest of our lives trying to be what God has declared that we are. You're salt and you're light. So be salty, give light. I really like these images because with salt and light there is this difference between the element and what's around it, but for the element to be effective it has to penetrate into that other realm.

One of my friends asked the question this way: Do you think that our problem is that we have too much world in the church or too little church in the world? Is the problem that we're so much like darkness and we've so much lost our saltiness that we no longer have an impact on the world, or is the problem that we're so withdrawn from the world that that salt and light is not having the impact that it should have?

The one thing that the wars in the Middle East have given us is a wonderful word. The word embedded. Embedded reporters. People who have planted themselves in the middle of a company of soldiers to see what it's really like. And when I read this passage now, I think about being embedded.

When we embed ourselves in the world, when we invest in the world, when we become deeply enmeshed in our culture, then and only then can we become salt and light in the world. More and more Christians seem to think that the only way that they can maintain their Christianity is withdraw from the world; but that's not the way salt and light works. It moves in, not away. So there are two issues here.

First, are we different enough from the world to make a difference in the world? God's declared us to be light. Are we then?

Second, is our light on a lamp stand? Are we a city on a hill? Are we so enmeshed and embedded in the world that the world actually has a chance to be influenced by the lives that we live?

The greatest personal evangelist I have ever known, the person who has led more people to a deep faith in Jesus Christ than any person I have ever known, claims to have never asked anyone for a Bible study. He is in the world in such a way that he is so salty and he is such light that he doesn't have to ask people to Bible studies. They ask him. Why do you live the way you do? What is it that makes you tick? Jesus says, "You are salt and light." That's who you are. You are the people who transform the world by your very presence. You're salt and light.

So now, I pronounce you salt and light.

And now we get to spend the rest of our lives trying to be what Jesus has declared us to be.

Discussing What Jesus Says
Read Matthew 5:13–16

If you are a follower of Jesus, he declares you to be salt and light.

In your experience, are Christians so separate from the world that they can't make any difference in the world?

Or have Christians become so much like the world that they're not different enough to make an impact on the world?

The images of salt and light have become part of the Christian vocabulary, but what does it really mean to be a city set on the hill or to be salt that changes the nature of the world?

Do you believe you are salt and light and making a difference in the world? Why or why not?

Doing What Jesus Says

Serve a meal to someone this week.

In every situation take the lowest place at a meal or table or celebration. Take the place of servant in every situation you are in this week.

If you are not used to wearing a cross, wear a cross necklace where it's visible so whatever you do becomes a visible sign of Jesus and your actions reflect on the cross.

Chapter Four

THE HEART
OF THE LAW
Matthew 5:17–20

Do not think that I have come to abolish the Law or the Prophets; I have not come to abolish them but to fulfill them. For truly I tell you, until heaven and earth disappear, not the smallest letter, not the least stroke of a pen, will by any means disappear from the Law until everything is accomplished. Therefore anyone who sets aside one of the least of these commands and teaches others accordingly will be called least in the kingdom of heaven, but whoever practices and teaches these commands will be called great in the kingdom of heaven. For I tell you that unless your righteousness surpasses that of the Pharisees and the teachers of the law, you will certainly not enter the kingdom of heaven.

When it comes to the way we view and practice the "Law of God," Christians have tended to fall into one of two groups. There are those we might call legalists who basically say Christianity is nothing more than keeping certain rules and regulations. There are others who so experience God's grace that they don't think there are any rules, that rules and laws don't matter anymore. Both miss the target Jesus sets up in the Sermon on the Mount.

Jesus says, "I've not come to abolish the law, I've come to fulfill it. In fact, not the least little bit of the law will be done away with until everything is fulfilled."

Really, Jesus! You didn't come to set me free from the law? In fact, Jesus shows us remarkable balance. You don't have to be a legalist, nor do you have to practice what Dietrich Bonhoeffer called "cheap grace" or grace without law, grace without discipleship. Jesus shows us what it means to practice the law in a way that's inside out, that's perfectly balanced.

A lot of people look at the Sermon on the Mount as Jesus' pitting his righteousness against the righteousness of the law. But Jesus makes it clear to us that he is not pitting his righteousness against the law. That's the wrong way to read it. Instead, Jesus is pitting his interpretation of the law against the way the Pharisees interpreted the law.

Jesus isn't pitting himself against the Law of Moses or Moses himself. No, he's countering certain ways of interpreting the law that were common among the Pharisees and teachers of the law in that time.

I had a friend tell me about going to his child's school and their bulletin board display was of all the things that they love. One student wrote the caption, "I love my dog," and the child drew an odd-shaped creature and you really hope that the family dog doesn't actually look like that.

And my friend sees another poster and the caption reads, "I love Torah."

What do you immediately know about that child? You know that this child who wrote, "I love Torah," is Jewish. Who else would say, "I love the law"?

Believe it or not, Jesus says, "I love Torah." He says, Don't think that I've come to abolish the Law and the Prophets. I haven't come to abolish them. I've come to fulfill them. In fact, I'm telling you the truth—not the smallest letter or stroke of a pen, none of that will disappear from the law until all has been fulfilled. Jesus says, I haven't come to tell you to be lawless; I want to give you a deeper understanding of the law.

Sometimes we think laws are restrictive, and I guess they are, but they're usually restrictive in really helpful ways. A friend told me recently about driving home from the northern part of the country in a blizzard, and it was absolutely whiteout conditions. He couldn't see the sides of the road. He couldn't see the center lane. There were no markers anywhere. It was a white-knuckle ride that ended well but could have been horrifying had he ended up in a ditch. If you've ever tried to drive in those conditions, you know that *any* marker you see that shows you the side of the road becomes your friend.

For Jesus, that's what Torah does. Torah is what keeps us in the lane. Torah is what keeps us from running off the road. Torah is your friend. And so the problem is not law. The problem is an interpretation that's too narrow or applied in a way that attempts to attain righteousness by law-keeping.

So in the heart of the Sermon on the Mount, Jesus addresses six different aspects of the keeping of Torah. In each one he tries to give us a deeper way of understanding. He begins by saying, "For I tell you that unless your righteousness surpasses that of the Pharisees and the teachers of the law, you will certainly not enter the kingdom of heaven."

Each of the six ways of keeping the law illustrate what Jesus means by righteousness that surpasses how the Pharisees and teachers of the law interpret and live it out. The key phrase Jesus uses six times is this: "You have heard it said." With this phase Jesus is not criticizing the law but rather the legalistic or immoral interpretation of the law.

In this chapter I will briefly sketch these six ways Jesus compared the way the Pharisees and law teachers interpreted the law with his own interpretation and what it means to "fulfill the law." Each of these six will be covered in more detail in the chapters that follow.

"You have heard that it was said to the people long ago, 'You shall not murder, and anyone who murders will be subject to judgment.' But I tell you that anyone who is angry with a brother or sister will be subject to judgment. Again, anyone who says to a brother or sister, 'Raca,' is answerable to the court. And anyone who says, 'You fool!' will be in danger of the fire of hell."

Jesus says, you have heard it said that you shall not murder, but I want to talk to you about anger. Jesus is so serious about relationships destroyed by anger that he elevates reconciliation above worship. He says, "Therefore, if you are offering your gift at the altar and there remember that your brother or sister has something against you, leave your gift there in front of the altar. First go and be reconciled to them; then come and offer your gift."

"You have heard that it was said, 'You shall not commit adultery.' But I tell you that anyone who looks at a woman lustfully has already committed adultery with her in his heart. If your right eye causes you to stumble, gouge it out and throw it away. It is better for you to lose one part of your body than for your whole body to be thrown into hell. And if your right hand causes you to stumble, cut it off and throw it away. It is better for you to lose one part of your body than for your whole body to go into hell."

Jesus says he wants to talk to us not just about committing adultery. He wants to talk to us about the lust that's in our hearts.

"It has been said, 'Anyone who divorces his wife must give her a certificate of divorce.' But I tell you that anyone who divorces his wife, except for sexual immorality, makes her the victim of adultery, and anyone who marries a divorced woman commits adultery."

Religious men thought all they had to do was do the paperwork right for divorce, and they could send their wives packing for any reason they pleased. But Jesus says, "I want to talk to you about deep faithfulness."

He says, "Again, you have heard that it was said to the people long ago, 'Do not break your oath, but fulfill to the Lord the vows you have made.' But I tell you, do not swear an oath at all: either by heaven, for it is God's throne; or by the earth, for it is his footstool; or by Jerusalem, for it is the city of the Great King. And do not swear by your head, for you cannot make even one hair white or black. All you need to say is simply 'Yes' or 'No'; anything beyond this comes from the evil one."

You have heard that it was said that if you swear by something important you have to keep your word; but I want you to have an integrity that goes so deep that no swearing that you would do would add anything to your word.

"You have heard that it was said, 'Eye for eye, and tooth for tooth.' But I tell you, do not resist an evil person. If anyone slaps you on the right cheek, turn to them the other cheek also. And if anyone wants to sue you and take your shirt, hand over your coat as well. If anyone forces you to go one mile, go with them two miles. Give to the one who asks you, and do not turn away from the one who wants to borrow from you."

There's a technical term for what Jesus is talking about: *lex talionis*. It means, "An eye for an eye a tooth for a tooth." The idea was to allow punishment for crimes without taking extra revenge. In the United States we have a similar idea that sounds a little more vanilla, but it means basically the same thing: let the punishment fit the crime. So Jesus is saying this: You have heard it said that if you're going to take revenge you can only take it in proportion to the crime that was committed; but I want to tell you, don't even start. Don't retaliate at all.

"You have heard that it was said, 'Love your neighbor and hate your enemy.' But I tell you, love your enemies and pray for those who persecute you, that you may be children of your Father in heaven. He causes his sun to rise on the evil and the good, and sends rain on the righteous and the unrighteous. If you love those who love you, what reward will you get? Are not even the tax collectors doing that? And if you greet only your own people, what are you doing more than others? Do not even pagans do that? Be perfect, therefore, as your heavenly Father is perfect."

You have heard it said that you should love those close to you but hate your enemies; but I tell you to love beyond your own tribe.

It's not a rejection of the law; it's a profound deepening of what the law means. It's not Jesus versus Torah. It's competing interpretations of what the law is about. I'm not very good at obeying rules and Jesus is going to show us that the key to obeying rules is doing it inside out. As long as we're trying to obey rules by just trying to make somebody happy who is pushing rules on us from the outside, we're always going to fail; but if the keeping of rules grows from inside, from our love of Torah, then all sorts of new life is possible to us. But this is hard because we have learned that grace means that rules aren't important or rules have no place in our lives.

But here Jesus says, "I want to talk to you about the law. Not only do I want you to keep it, I want you to keep it in deeper ways than you've ever imagined before."

One of the reasons why I have such a hard time obeying rules is because I'm right about everything. I know best. And when you're obedient you're actually having to submit to another person; and it's very hard to submit to other people when you know better than they do. How am I going to submit or obey when I always know what's right? But Jesus comes along and says, "I am the authoritative interpreter of Torah. Do you want to pit your wisdom, Randy, against mine? Do you really think that you know better than I do about how life ought to be ordered?" And so this really becomes an act of submission.

What about you? Do you believe that Jesus is the one who can show us how to order our lives correctly?

Being a college professor, one of the things I get to do is watch the devolvement of the English language. Those were "the good old days" when good meant good and bad meant bad, but somewhere along the line bad came to mean really good and the only way you can tell the difference between bad that was bad and bad that was good was the inflection, and I never could quite get it. Apparently when something was bad it means it's really good. And then it really got worse when I found out that sick means something that's really bad which means it is way good.

What Jesus talks to us about here is sick, bad righteousness. Righteousness that goes all the way to the ground floor. Deep, inner righteousness that leads to a way of life. That's not legalism. That's Jesus' way. So in the next six sections Jesus is going to show us what it means to live sick, bad righteousness, to have a life where our goodness goes all the way to the bottom, and this he calls the fulfillment of Torah. When we come to understand that, then we can say with that child who made the poster, "I love Torah!" Because Torah shows us the heart of God, and as his heart becomes our heart, obeying the law becomes a profound act of grace.

Someday the practice of saying that something good is "sick" or "bad" will go out of style; but what Jesus says will never go out of style. He says do not set these laws aside. If you do and teach others to do so, you will be called least in the kingdom. Jesus continues, *"but whoever practices and teaches these commands will be called great in the kingdom of heaven."* I do not want to set aside one of the least of these commands and teach others to do the same. I don't want to be called "least in the kingdom of heaven." With all my heart I want to practice and teach these commands. And even though I practice them imperfectly, Jesus promises that the ones who practice these commands and teach others to do likewise will be called "great in the kingdom of heaven."

Like many things in life, this is so much easier said than done! To reach a place where we experience grace and also practice the commands of Jesus is a balancing act that will take a lifetime to learn and grow in. Do you have trouble with this balance in your life? I have trouble finding balance in life. I accept grace without discipleship. I indulge in grace without commitment—cheap grace. Grace without sacrifice and in fact grace without death. When Jesus calls us to come and follow him, he calls us to a way of following the law that requires everything that we have. It goes all the way down. It's not just keeping a bunch of rules and regulations. It's a remaking of our hearts.

Jesus says that when we read the law what we find out is what God cares about, what's in his heart, and he intends for all of it to be fulfilled in our lives. Legalism has been a problem in Christianity. There's no question that some people's understanding of Christianity is that it is nothing more than a bunch of rules and regulations that have to be kept, but in some ways an even bigger threat has been our unwillingness to place ourselves under the discipline of the law as Jesus understands it. He calls us to live this out all the way down to the core of our being, so that our lives become a reflection of the heart of God.

Do you have trouble finding balance like I do? Sometimes when I listen to myself I think, *You talk too much about rules and regulations.* Other times when I listen to myself I think, *You're not calling people to deep discipleship the way Jesus did.* But as in all things, Jesus is our teacher here and he shows us this perfect balance—how to be serious about living out the law and at the same time having it be a heart response not just a response to a checklist.

Jesus becomes our teacher and he shows us balance in our lives.

Discussing What Jesus Says
Read Matthew 5:17–20

One of the keys to interpreting the Sermon on the Mount is this: your life should be better than the works righteousness practiced by people like the Pharisees.

Jesus says when we read the law what we find out is what God cares about. What does God care about?

Does following Jesus mean more about rules and regulations or does it mean calling people to living out deep discipleship?

Are you willing to put yourself under the discipline of the law the way Jesus sees it?

Doing What Jesus Says

For each of ten days in a row, take one of the Ten Commandments and go to the heart of the principle behind the command and try to practice it that day. Look for the deeper principle in that command of God.

Chapter Five

Idiot! Stupid! Moron!
Matthew 5:21–26

You have heard that it was said to the people long ago, 'You shall not murder, and anyone who murders will be subject to judgment.' But I tell you that anyone who is angry with a brother or sister will be subject to judgment. Again, anyone who says to a brother or sister, 'Raca,' is answerable to the court. And anyone who says, 'You fool!' will be in danger of the fire of hell.

Therefore, if you are offering your gift at the altar and there remember that your brother or sister has something against you, leave your gift there in front of the altar. First go and be reconciled to them; then come and offer your gift.

Settle matters quickly with your adversary who is taking you to court. Do it while you are still together on the way, or your adversary may hand you over to the judge, and the judge may hand you over to the officer, and you may be thrown into prison. Truly I tell you, you will not get out until you have paid the last penny.

Idiot. Stupid. Moron.

And those are just the ones I can put in print.

How many of these words have exited your mouth in the last week?

In Jesus day it was "Raca" and "You fool!" These were the ways people showed utter disrespect and tore others down.

In one of the great novels of the twenty-first century, Roberto Bolaño's *2666*, he tells the horrific tale of twenty years of murders, rapes, and torturing of young women. That part of the book is true. It occurred in an area of Mexico, and the crime was never solved for twenty years. It went on and on and on.

At one point in the book some detectives who are supposed to be working on the case are sitting in a bar and telling what, for what lack of a better term, we would call "blond jokes." They're making fun of women, and Bolaño wants us to see a key point: these jokes and these murders have something to do with each other.

It begins with disrespect for women and it ends in murder.

And Jesus says the same thing in the Sermon on the Mount. What ends in murder begins with murderous thoughts.

We've become experts at sarcasm and insults. We are expert at destroying relationships, but we all know it is a lot easier to destroy a relationship than it is to restore one. It begins with disrespect, with demeaning, with degrading.

In this section of the Sermon on the Mount, Jesus shows us a way different from the way of insults, sarcasm, and murderous thoughts. He shows us another way: the way of reconciliation, the way of building and not destroying. In a world like ours where relationships are so easily destroyed and so hard to rebuild, we need to hear Jesus' good word on this.

Idiot.

Moron.

Stupid.

It's so easy to tear down. So hard to rebuild.

When Jesus starts off by saying, "You have heard that it was said, 'You shall not murder,'" I feel pretty good about myself, because I haven't killed anybody all day, and I think I've got a decent chance of getting through the day without killing anybody.

But then Jesus says, "But I say to you, anyone who is angry with his brother is in danger of judgment." And if I'm doing pretty well on the murder side, I'm not doing quite as well on the anger side.

I was teaching the Sermon on the Mount to a really huge freshman class, and we were coming to this section. In this class I had students from all different majors. I had people who had been in Christian schools all their lives, and I had people who didn't know the difference between a chapter and a verse in the Bible.

So I'm always thinking, *How am I going to teach this passage?*

So as I'm coming in the room, I have this great idea. I see a student—I'll call him Joe—sitting at the back of the room, and I go and sit beside Joe and I say, "Can you act?"

Joe says, "Act? What do you mean?"

"You know, act."

"You mean like *drama?*"

"Yeah, like drama," I said.

"Of course not, why?"

"I need a student to act as if he is so angry with me that we can convince the class that we are going to get in a physical altercation," I said.

He thought about this and decided that wasn't such a stretch, that perhaps he could do it.

So I said, "Okay, this is what I want you to do. I'm going to make a big deal out of telling the class to shut off their cell phones like I always do and then in the middle of my lecture I want you to make your cell phone go off, really loudly, and I'm going to come after you and I don't want you to back off and we're going to try to convince the class that we're going to have a fight."

Joe says, "That will never work."

"It will if you don't over act," I said. "And at no point are you to touch me."

So I start lecturing, and a few minutes into my lecture he makes his cell phone go off really loudly. I had made a big deal about telling everybody to shut off their cell phones, so I look up and there's this nervous laughter out there. It's an awkward moment. I slam my Bible shut and start walking in his direction, and I look at him and I say, "Is that your cell phone?"

And he was great. He said, "Yeah it was, I'm sorry, I didn't mean for that to happen. I apologize."

And I said, "What was there about the words 'turn off your cell phone' that you didn't understand? Those are all one syllable words. Even though you're an athlete, you should have been able to understand that!"

And Joe was great. He didn't raise his voice. He just folded his arms, looked at me and said, "What is your problem?"

"Well, right now, you are," I said.

He says, "I can solve that for you," and Joe starts to pile up his stuff and walk out of the room. And so I march up the aisle after him and I yell at him, "The next step you take had better be towards me."

He turned and stopped right there in front of my face. You could have heard a pin drop. I now have two hundred and fifty freshmen and ten teaching assistants who all think we're getting ready to get into a fight. It was so convincing that an international student sitting in the class still thinks it was totally real.

About that time I throw my arm around the student, and I look at the class and say, "Gotcha!"

But they don't laugh. Nothing but silence and stares. It was totally crickets chirping.

They were so disturbed that it took a full five minutes before I could get them to see how hilarious this was. After I got them calmed down, I said, "Okay, why did you believe that?"

"Have I done *anything* in the last six weeks that would make you think I would react that way?"

I said, "Let me tell you why you believed it. This is why: Because the whole world is crazy. That's why you believed it. We are all so defensive, so angry, that when somebody goes off like that it is easy to believe because that's the world we live in."

I travel a lot. I meet a lot of Christians and I have to tell you that, as a group, they are some of the angriest people I know. And if you ask me what Christians are angry about, the answer is... yes. They're just angry in principle. And Jesus says murder begins in anger. Congratulations on not killing anybody. How you doing with your anger?

But let's come back to these unusual words Jesus uses in the text where he says, "If you say to your brother 'Raca!' you're in danger of judgment." Jesus is basically saying, if you say to a person "You idiot!" it raises questions about their intelligence; and then he says, if you say to a person, "You fool!" you are in danger of hell. Unfortunately in this book there's no way I can accurately translate "You fool!'" without it getting edited out. I'd have to use profanity to duplicate the impact of the words Jesus used—words that cut at the very essence of a person's worth.

That's what anger does. Chops people down. Tears them down. Raises questions about their worth as a person. And Jesus says, let me tell you how seriously I take this.

He says, if you're on your way to worship and you remember that your brother has something against you, this is so important that I want you to forget about worship and I want you first to go and be reconciled to your brother or sister before you even think about coming to worship. That's how important this is.

That our relationships are governed by respect and reconciliation and love, Jesus says, is far more important than anything that could possibly happen in worship. So what if we replaced our anger with a passion for reconciliation so that we become the peacemakers upon whom Jesus pronounces a blessing?

Can you imagine what the world would look like if everybody would lay down their anger. You know, you don't find very many Christians who will say, "I think that my relationships are more important than my worship, and I can't imagine going to worship while I have these unreconciled relationships out there."

Throughout the Sermon on the Mount Jesus is going to talk about these ever escalating cycles of violence and retribution. Over and over again he talks about how things roll and roll and roll and how you have to cut it off at the beginning. The way you prevent murder, the way you prevent war, the way you prevent violence, the way you prevent tribalism is cutting it out at the root. Congratulations on not killing anybody. How you doing with your anger?

Or what about trash talking? It's part of the great American sport. Some of the great trash talking of all time happens on sports fields and courts. Athletes and fans are some of the greatest trash talkers ever.

But trash talking doesn't stop at the foul poles and penalty boxes. The foul balls go much further than home plate. Christians can talk trash with the best of them. Some of the great trash talking of all time comes out of laptop and tablet computers in Christian homes and offices and is heard in the halls of churches and Christian organizations.

But Jesus makes it clear to us that trash talking can be serious business. He says there are ways of talking about people that aren't just playful, they're hurtful and damaging, and then he calls us to engage in reconciling relationships—and to Jesus that is so important that it trumps worship.

Christians have always thought that worship was so important, but to Jesus the relationships we have with people are more important than offering one's sacrifice at the altar.

One of my favorite movies—one that virtually no one has seen—is called *Forgiving Dr. Mengele.* It's about a Jewish woman who was a victim of Dr. Mengele's experiments during the holocaust. Mengele had long been dead, but she decided she wanted to forgive him because, until she did, he still had control of her life. And it was amazing how much opposition she got from all those around her—that it was unthinkable that she would forgive him. But she knew the power of forgiveness.

There's somebody out there with whom you need to be reconciled. And until you practice that reconciliation, the power of forgiveness is never fully present in your life.

Oh, trash talk is easy. It's easy to tear down. It's a lot harder to build up and to restore, so Jesus says it's not about murder, it's about murderous thoughts. It's about demeaning another person. It's about tearing them down. But that's not the way it has to be in our world. We can start today on the cycle of reconciliation where relationships are restored and not destroyed, where friendships are deepened, not demeaned.

Who are you thinking about right now? Who is it that you want to restore a relationship with? It's time we start an epidemic of reconciliation.

Discussing What Jesus Says
Read Matthew 5:21–26

Words are weapons of mass destruction, but they can also be used to rebuild relationships.

What are ways we might begin with degrading thoughts, move to hateful thoughts, then end up with murderous thoughts?

Why is it easier to destroy than to build?

What have you done to restore a relationship in the last ten years?

Doing What Jesus Says

The Sermon on the Mount is to be lived, so I have a challenge for you. There are people out there with whom you need to be reconciled.

It may be your fault.

It may be their fault.

You may not know whose fault it is.

But Jesus challenges us to restore those relationships. It is much easier to destroy than it is to reconcile.

Identify people with whom you have unreconciled relationships. Make some effort toward reconciliation or start approaching, and do it in such a way that doesn't blame the other person.

Chapter Six

GOD MADE SEX REALLY GOOD
Matthew 5:27–32

You have heard that it was said, 'You shall not commit adultery.' But I tell you that anyone who looks at a woman lustfully has already committed adultery with her in his heart. If your right eye causes you to stumble, gouge it out and throw it away. It is better for you to lose one part of your body than for your whole body to be thrown into hell. And if your right hand causes you to stumble, cut it off and throw it away. It is better for you to lose one part of your body than for your whole body to go into hell.

It has been said, 'Anyone who divorces his wife must give her a certificate of divorce.' But I tell you that anyone who divorces his wife, except for sexual immorality, makes her the victim of adultery, and anyone who marries a divorced woman commits adultery.

It's hard to imagine people living in the fifth century. And it may come as a shock to you that a guy with a name like Augustine, who was a powerful voice of early Christianity and lived in a place called Hippo, really wrestled with something that most of us struggle with today.

Augustine the Bishop of Hippo was the single most important voice in Christianity for a thousand years beginning in 430 AD. And Augustine the Bishop of Hippo struggled with sexual desire. He converted to Christianity as an adult and carried into his Christian life a lot of baggage of sexual sin. In his writings, he made a virtual equivalence between sex and sin, and the church inherited this view. It has persisted for centuries in the Christian tradition.

In Scripture, sex and sin are far from the same thing. The Bible teaches that sex can be practiced in a sinful and immoral way, but also shows sex to be one of the basic building blocks of our humanity. From the story of creation all the way to the hot, erotic poetry of Song of Solomon, sexuality is created by God who looks at it and declares it to be good.

In the Sermon on the Mount, Jesus notices that sexuality can, and often does, go wrong. And in our culture, not only has it gone wrong, it has gone badly wrong.

As I noted in a previous chapter, Jesus contrasts a religious cultural view with his interpretation of the law. "You've heard that it was said you shall not commit adultery, but I tell you, anyone who looks at a woman lustfully has already committed adultery."

Wow, that makes you wonder: Is there anybody in the world who's not an adulterer? President Jimmy Carter famously said, "I've looked on many women with lust. I've committed adultery in my heart many times. God knows I will do this and forgives me." Some thought he was crazy for saying such a thing. To the ears of those who haven't heard the words of Jesus in the Sermon on the Mount, Carter's confession was unbelievable in at least two ways. First: Who doesn't think about sex? Who doesn't lust? And second: Are you kidding me? You've never had a physical sexual indiscretion? But most people didn't know that Carter's confession was based on practicing the radical purity set by Jesus in the Sermon on the Mount.

Jesus talks about sex in profound ways. And he works out of this rich Old Testament background. Sometimes we've been so influenced by Greek thought that we miss the rich Jewish notion that all things created by God are good, and that means sex is good. Or, if you want to listen to Song of Solomon, sex is way good.

Clyde Edgerton's novel *Killer Diller* tells the story of a young man who is an ex-convict; he's converted by an elderly Christian woman and goes to a Christian college. And one of the great parts of the book is when he reads Song of Solomon for the first time. It comes as a revelation to him and he goes to the older woman and says, "I have been reading Song of Solomon and it is hot!"

The woman who converted the man says, "I don't think so."

The ex-convict convert says, "Oh, yes, it's hot."

"No, I think that's about Christ and the church."

And he says, "Have you read it?"

It sizzles. It's hot. If you're under eighteen, you shouldn't read it. Sex is good.

But Jesus is concerned. He's concerned with lust. And how concerned is he? This is how serious it is. If your eye is giving you offense, if your eye is causing you to lust, cut it out. Cut off your hands if they cause you to sin.

What is he talking about? It's clearly hyperbolic language, but Jesus says this is so serious that you may have to take extreme measures. If you look at a woman for the purpose of lusting, you are already committing adultery, so take extreme measures to stay away from places and situations where you might lust. And this comes to the heart of the matter.

The deep sin attached to lust and pornography is that you use another person as simply an object of your desires. It's the ultimate selfish act. The other person doesn't matter at all except as a means to fulfill your own desires. And that objectification of another person is a violation of their fundamental dignity, and that's why Jesus says there's no room here for lust.

I remember a young couple who were married and he was going through what I would describe as delayed adolescent jerkdom—some stuff he should have gone through earlier in life. While his wife was in the house, he was watching pornography. I'm not saying he should have been watching it when she was away or anytime. And they were having this debate about whether this constituted adultery or not. I suggested she just hit him with a hammer. This is a meaningless debate. This is about the quality of heart, about objectifying another person, about seeing that other person with worth and dignity beyond your desires. That's why lust and pornography are so sinister in our world.

And piled right on behind this discussion of adultery, Jesus says a couple of quick sentences about divorce. He says you've heard it was said that if you're going to get a divorce you have to give a certificate of divorce, but I tell you, anyone who divorces his wife commits adultery. Jesus says that what holds people together is so sacred that to divide it up commits fundamental sin; and in a world of throw away marriages, his words ring hard in our ears. He really means this—that getting a divorce is tantamount to adultery. I wonder if both divorce and adultery are out of the same framework. Jesus says as long as you're preoccupied with your own needs, when the other person is only an object to fulfill your needs, then when that spouse stops fulfilling needs in the way you want, then you'll throw him or her away and get another one. That's the same sort of objectification you do with that person you use as the object of your lust.

One of my favorite Christian authors, Sheldon Vanauken, a friend of C. S. Lewis, said years ago that when you get a new car you should also get a hammer. Take that hammer and go out and put the first dent in the brand new car yourself. Then you're not afraid to use it anymore. That way you don't have to park at the end of the parking lot to protect from door dings, because you've already put the first dent in it yourself. Vanauken's point was this: things are not to be loved, they're to be used. The corollary to that is this: people are not to be used, they're to be loved.

It is amazing how much time we spend loving and caring for things and using people. What would happen if we took seriously the fact that things are to be used and not loved and people are to be loved and not used?

I'm really grateful that I grew up when I did. Pornography was available when I was a young person, but you had to work to get it. You had to take chances. You had to take risks. You could get caught.

Today, pornography is available at the push of a link on the internet. It's "anonymous" and you can get it whenever you want. We've created a whole society that thinks that people are out there to fulfill their desires. And we've created a world where, if a spouse doesn't fulfill my needs anymore, they're a throwaway item.

Jesus calls us back to a different view of the world where people are to be loved, not used, where faithfulness is a deep and powerful characteristic of our lives. One can't help but admire a beautiful woman or handsome man, but you glance, you appreciate, you think how God is a great creator. It's when we take that next step and we linger and we desire and we use that person, not as a person but as a thing—that is the sin of lust.

Can you imagine a world where we put that away, where we really loved people with integrity for who they are and stopped using them as objects of our own fulfillment? I don't know about you, but that's a world I'd love to live in.

How is it that one of the greatest gifts of God's love, human sexuality, has gone so wrong in our world? In our sex-crazed world, sex is everywhere. We might blame technology for part of it. Sex is now available anytime, anyplace, and anonymously, but long before the internet came along, human beings were already struggling with God's good gift. Even in the time of Jesus he understood that sexuality was not only a great gift of God, but also a gift capable of being perverted in serious and destructive ways. Of course, Jesus shows us that the real problem is not that we can't control ourselves sexually, but that we have a problem on the inside, the problem of the human heart.

When we were shooting the video companion to this book, we visited a house that looked really good on the outside, but was totally rotten on the inside. This illustrates the heart problem we have when it comes to sex. And so Jesus addresses the question, not just of adultery, but also of lust. He understands that this is one of those problems that can only be solved from the inside out. In his hyperbolic statement about plucking out one's eye or cutting off one's hand, he does point out that one has to control input. You can't fill your life with images that create lust in you and expect to remain pure. In the long run this problem can't be solved from the outside in.

Certainly external boundaries help us to remain pure. Using an internet filter or using the computer in a public place helps guard us from lust, but ultimately lust can only be solved from the inside out.

Ed Dobson tells a story in his book, *A Year of Living Like Jesus*, about a student who came to him after a lecture at a Christian university in Florida. The young man had one eye, and he said he actually took Jesus' statement to pluck out his eye quite literally. He poked out his own eye because he was lusting! Dobson stood dumbfounded, unable to believe he had truly met someone who had done what Jesus said in this area of lust. But that's when the young man said something he would never forget. He said he followed what Jesus said, he'd plucked out his eye . . . but now he is still tempted to lust with one eye.

We have to change the way we look at the world. We have to change the way we look at people. We have to change our hearts. Plucking out our eyes and cutting off our hands won't change our hearts. Like the student, we might just become one-eyed lusters.

And finally, what's at the heart of most sexual sin, whether pornography or adultery, is that we use the other person as a means to our own gratification instead of caring about the other person as a person. We simply use him or her to fulfill our sexual desire. In other words, the heart of sexual sin is always selfishness. And it's this sin that Jesus says must be cut out at the roots. We have to look and see people in a different way: as fellow human beings created in the image of God, as people worthy of our respect, not as objects to fulfill our desires.

I work with eighteen- to twenty-two-year-olds and they struggle with sexual sin all the time. The things we talk about are these:

1. If you want to cut something off, cut off the input of pornography and tempting situations.
2. You have to get a community of support.
3. You have to trust God to remake your heart.
4. You start to think in different ways and when you do that, sex becomes, not just manageable, but again becomes the good gift that God gave. In Paul's words, "whatsoever is pure, dwell on these things." Think about things that inspire, that change your heart to be closer to God's heart, and that keep you thinking of people as humans and not objects. Think about things that lead you to God.
5. Learn to express love the way God intended, not simply as a way of fulfilling your own selfish desires. Jesus' instruction on this would remake our world which has fallen off the cliff when it comes to sexuality.

Discussing What Jesus Says
Read Matthew 5:27–32

Sex truly is God's idea from the beginning and humanity has found ways to corrupt it.

What is badly wrong in our culture when it comes to sexuality?

In what ways has sex and sin been viewed as equivalent in church teachings you've experienced?

In what ways do you objectify or diminish the humanity of other people that you know or don't know?

Is there something you need to confess to a spouse, a girlfriend, boyfriend, or fiancé?

How can you develop a protection for your heart from the "second look" of lust?

Doing What Jesus Says

Refer to the list of suggestions at the end of the chapter.

Do not use sexually suggestive humor or language. Walk away when it's used.

Stay away from all forms of media, computer, television, movies that tend to feature lust.

Pay particular attention to treat everyone, members of the opposite sex in particular, with respect

Divorce—think about what Jesus says about divorce and practice covenant keeping in everything you do. The "small" ways we do not keep covenant bleed into our "big" covenants, like marriage.

So keep track for a period time of how many times you've made a promise—no matter how trivial—and broken it. If you make a promise or say you'll do something, be sure you keep that promise or commitment.

Then see how many times you make promises you don't fulfill. Do you ever say, "I'll pray for you" and never pray for that person seriously, or ever? Have you over-extended yourself so that you can't keep your commitments well? The Church of the Savior uses this language: "If you are over-extended you are under-committed." If you say you'll be there at a certain time and date, are you there? Do you think you are reliable? What do other people think about you? Do people see you as reliable?

Chapter Seven

DEEP INTEGRITY
Matthew 5:33–37

Again, you have heard that it was said to the people long ago, 'Do not break your oath, but fulfill to the Lord the vows you have made.' But I tell you, do not swear an oath at all: either by heaven, for it is God's throne; or by the earth, for it is his footstool; or by Jerusalem, for it is the city of the Great King. And do not swear by your head, for you cannot make even one hair white or black. All you need to say is simply 'Yes' or 'No'; anything beyond this comes from the evil one.

Like a lot of teachers, I'm bothered by the studies that show one after another that virtually every student cheats. Not every student cheats on everything, but almost all of them say at some time in their college career that they cheat. They take the shortcut. They lie. They're dishonest.

A few years ago *Time* magazine ran a cover article that read, "Lying: Everybody's Doing It." And the article just observed how prevalent dishonesty and lying had become in American public life. It's gotten to the point now where we don't even expect people to be honest.

A group of behavioral economists did a really interesting study. They created a test where people were encouraged to cheat so that they could make more money by getting more answers right. They then divided their group up into two, and in one group they had them write all of the Ten Commandments they could remember before they took the test and the other group they had write the recent movies they had seen. And what they found was really interesting. When these groups of people took the test and again were encouraged to cheat, what they found is that those who had written the Ten Commandments actually cheated far less than the other group—and it didn't matter how many of the Ten Commandments they could remember. Just by thinking about those commands their desire to cheat went down.

Deep Integrity

It appears that we basically believe that we ought to tell the truth and be honest, but sometimes that's not the operative story we live by. That was true in Jesus day, too.

In this section of the Sermon on the Mount, Jesus talks about our need for this deep integrity that goes all the way to the bottom and how there's always the great temptation to fudge or in some situations not to tell the truth because we don't think it's that important. Well, if we're going to be serious followers of Jesus, then telling the truth and nothing but the truth suddenly becomes a really important part of our lives.

Jesus says you have heard that you shall not break your oaths, but keep the oaths you have made to the Lord. But he says don't swear at all. Don't swear by heaven. Don't swear by the earth. Don't swear by Jerusalem. Don't swear by your head. And because of that language, we tend to think that this passage is about swearing or taking an oath; some people have read this passage and decided that it means that they can't swear to tell the truth in court, which by the way is a handy interpretation. But this passage is not about swearing.

The passage is about integrity. Everybody knows that when you're a kid there is a way to tell a lie and that lie doesn't count. What do you do? You cross your fingers. By the way, there's a statute of limitations on that! After you get past age eighteen, crossing your fingers doesn't work anymore. So this passage is about the ancient practice of crossing your fingers. If I say something to you and I don't swear by anything important, then I don't have to tell the truth. I only have to tell the truth when I swear by something important. And so the passage is not really about not swearing. The passage is about telling the truth; it is about having integrity.

Jesus says, "What I'm telling you is you shouldn't swear at all. That is, no oath that you take should be able to add anything to your word. Just let your yes be yes and your no be no; anything else comes from the evil one." In other words, I want you to have an integrity that runs so deep that nothing you could say would add anything to your simple word.

I want you to think about our language. One of my favorite words in English is "really." I'll tell you a story and you'll say, "Really." Meaning, maybe what I told you was true and maybe it wasn't. Jesus wants to put that "really" out of business. When I say something you don't have to say "Really?" or "Is that true?" because it's always true. There are times when integrity is easy, but integrity really proves itself when it's hard. I have a test that I give to my students to find out if they have integrity. I'm pretty sure they don't, but it's important that they know they don't.

My students are very harsh and very critical of public figures who get in trouble and then try to lie their way out of it. And so I got to wondering whether my students would do any better. So I tried to create a dilemma where I was pretty sure they would lie. And here it is.

While I'm telling this story, I want you to sit in the class with them and imagine you are there, squarely in the middle of this dilemma and answer for yourself. What would you do?

I tell my students the following story.

Suppose it's your last semester at school, and you're getting ready to graduate with a degree in accounting. You have a person who's ready to marry you. You have a job lined up with one of the few accounting firms that's still left in the world. Life is perfect. And then you get the dreaded call from the registrar's office. You're one course short of graduation. You complain. You cry. You try to negotiate, but if you don't know this you should: it is easier to negotiate with a terrorist than it is with a registrar. You finally just give up and say, "What do I have to do?" You have to take an English class. So you take the only English class that fits into your schedule, early American literature.

The first thing you read is *The Scarlet Letter*. Have you read *The Scarlet Letter*? It's a fascinating book. It is all about sex but still manages to be deadly boring. Leave it to a Puritan to take the most salacious of possible topics and make it boring! After you get through that loser, you read Huckleberry Finn and you're delighted about that because you didn't know it was literature. Then you get to the poetry. None of it rhymes. The great thing about poetry is that it's short. You're not doing great but you're managing. And then you come to the last assignment in the course, which is to read the great American novel, and everyone knows this is *Moby Dick*.

For those of you who don't know this, *Moby Dick* is eight hundred dense pages about whaling. You're from Kansas. Whales haven't been an important part of your life. You're thinking they're not going to be. You're thinking, *I've been a good sport up until now, but I am not reading Moby Dick!*

So you begin to prepare otherwise. You first of all read the Cliff Notes or the Monarch Notes, because you figure whoever writes the notes would understand the book better than you would have anyway. But you don't stop there. You watch both movies—the one with Gregory Peck and the one with the Star Trek guy. You're not expecting to get an "A" in this class or on this test, you just want to get your "C" and get on with your life.

You come to the test, the final test in the course, and this idiot of a professor has put only one question on the final test.

That question on the test—the one and only question is this: Did you read *Moby Dick*?

And if you answer that question truthfully, you will get a zero on the final. You will fail the course. You won't graduate. You won't get that job you've lined up, and that person who was going to marry you is probably not going to marry a loser like you.

Would you tell the truth in that situation?

I've given that dilemma to students for years. It's really interesting. Some students I didn't think could think at all suddenly became theologians. Oooohhh. They think God is timeless so I can say I read the book, read it later, and it will be the same to God! Ninety-five percent of my students say in that situation of course they would lie and then begin to explain to me why that would be the right thing to do. Melville's dead. It's a victimless crime. God wants me to marry that person. He wants me to get that good job so I can give my money to the poor. I'm strongly suspecting that the five percent of the people who say they wouldn't lie are probably lying about that. Isn't that interesting?

What about you? What would you have done?

For most of us, when it comes down to it, if the cost is high enough, our integrity is for sale. But if we go through the rest of our lives deciding whether we're going to tell the truth or not based on cost benefit analysis, we're going to lie a lot. I don't know if you've noticed, but we've got an integrity crisis in the world.

When Jesus comes along and says I want you to have an integrity that runs so deep that when you say yes it always means yes and when you say no it always means no—that is teaching that would revolutionize the world.

I heard a well-known Christian speaker in chapel at a school far away, and I was really excited about hearing him. He got up and said he wanted to talk to us about integrity. You know I really got excited because I'm an ethics teacher.

The speaker began by saying, "Okay, we're going to talk about integrity." He said, "I talked to the three most successful people I know, and I asked them, 'To what do you attribute your success?'"

All three of these highly successful people said the same thing: integrity. They attributed their success to integrity. The speaker was very excited about this correlation, but I was not happy. Why? What's the downside to what he was saying? How could I be so negative?

Sitting on the front row I thought, *Oh, you will never recover from that.* Because you've told the students the right thing but given them the wrong reason for doing it. You've told them the reason they ought to have integrity is because it leads to success. Anybody can have integrity when it leads to success. The question is will we have integrity when it leads to the cross?

So Jesus says there's no point in swearing. You need to be so much like your Father in heaven that yes means yes and no means no and truthfulness is our way of life and the reason we're not going to cheat on the *Moby Dick* test is this: because we're not that kind of people. We're people who have been formed from the Sermon on the Mount and we understand this. Yes has to mean yes and no has to mean no. At least that's Jesus' opinion.

I think you see how difficult it is. If the stakes are high enough to fudge the truth when it doesn't really seem as if there's any difference, and if we make our decisions based on cost benefit analysis, there's going to be a lot of dishonesty. One of the things I'm really curious about is, Do you think that integrity is something you can "sort of" have? Not according to Jesus. He says our yes should mean yes and no mean no. At some point we've got to decide if we're going to tell the truth because that's what it means to be a follower of Jesus Christ. And even in situations where it may cost us enormously, yes means yes and no means no, because that's what Jesus calls us to do.

Discussing What Jesus Says
Read Matthew 5:33–37

Have integrity so deep that no oath or promise or stack of Bibles can add truth to your words.

If your final grade in the last class you needed to graduate from college came down to one question of honesty: Did you read Moby Dick? would you be tempted to say you read it, even though you really only read the Cliff Notes and saw the movie?

If there's a high enough price, is your integrity for sale?

What are you doing about the integrity crisis in the world?

Are you only honest when it leads to success? What about when it makes you look bad?

Is integrity something you can "sort of" have?

Doing What Jesus Says

At the first hint of falsehood (a slight misleading or a blatant lie) immediately seek to rectify it. If it can't be done right away, do it within one hour. Until you have done this, do your best not to speak to anyone.

Contact a friend or family member every other night/day for the next two weeks for reflection and confession. Confess the exact nature of your wrongs. And reflect with each other on why it is that you think you are lying.

The goal here is to examine our hearts and to expose the roots of our dishonesty.

Determine the time(s) of day when you are tempted to have the least integrity. Is it late at night? Mid-afternoon with no one in the room? Set up a plan with a friend or family member to be in contact during these times for encouragement and prayer.

For two weeks, do not use the word "maybe" unless absolutely necessary.

At the job or in school, do not waste time on the clock doing Facebook or texting unnecessarily: this is stealing from your employer or teacher. Ask your boss what else can be done.

Chapter Eight

HOLY
PRANK!
Matthew 5:38–48

You have heard that it was said, 'Eye for eye, and tooth for tooth.' But I tell you, do not resist an evil person. If anyone slaps you on the right cheek, turn to them the other cheek also. And if anyone wants to sue you and take your shirt, hand over your coat as well. If anyone forces you to go one mile, go with them two miles. Give to the one who asks you, and do not turn away from the one who wants to borrow from you.

You have heard that it was said, 'Love your neighbor and hate your enemy.' But I tell you, love your enemies and pray for those who persecute you, that you may be children of your Father in heaven. He causes his sun to rise on the evil and the good, and sends rain on the righteous and the unrighteous. If you love those who love you, what reward will you get? Are not even the tax collectors doing that? And if you greet only your own people, what are you doing more than others? Do not even pagans do that? Be perfect, therefore, as your heavenly Father is perfect.

Violence and conflict have been part of the human experience from the beginning.

Historically, societies have attempted to deal with this violence and conflict through the rule of law. Judges preside over courtrooms in order to deal with the chaos we find in our world. There is even a phrase we all know when those in a courtroom descend into disorder and misbehavior: The judge says firmly, "Order in the court!"

The judge often has to say, "Order in the court!" more than once when feathers get ruffled. I wonder if any amount of quieting by a judge can overcome the heart of revenge in people in a courtroom. This difficulty to still even the most basic outbursts leads me to wonder about these courtrooms and judges. Some courts and judges do justice and much good, but how well does the presence of judges and courtrooms work to decrease violence and chaos in our world today?

Put more simply, does the court system reduce violence?

This chapter is not a discourse about the effectiveness of the United States judicial branch. I'm posing this question to get at something Jesus was getting at in the Sermon on the Mount.

Sure, judges and prosecutors convict people and either send them to jail or execute them, but we continue to see, year after year, an increase in violence and conflict in our world. Why is this? Is there something bound up in the heart of humanity that no law or court can extract?

I think the answer is yes. There is something in the heart that laws and courts can never fully address or deal with effectively. This doesn't render the courts useless. But it does render them limited.

But we still have hope, because Jesus offers us another way. He offers us the way of non-retaliation and love for enemies rather than getting even and obsessing about revenge, even through the courts. Jesus offers a way different from loving only those who are members of our own ethnic group or particular party or tribe.

What would happen in our personal relationships if we accepted Jesus' way instead of trying to get even? What would happen if, instead of loving only those who love us, we accepted his ethic of universal love, even for our enemies?

Accepting this ethic is hard, even when we're playing around. Have you ever gone to camp? There is a lot of revenge at camp. Often healthy cabin competition goes awry, and the activity I'm thinking about usually involves revenge between cabins that escalates. One cabin does something disgusting to another cabin. Boys' cabins are particularly good at the disgusting part. And this disgusting part usually involves a smell. This, of course, is just the opening salvo, because once you have done something to another cabin, they simply must get even, if they are a self-respecting, unified cabin. Not only do they have to do something to your cabin, they have to do something to your cabin that is slightly worse than what you did to theirs. But then they're ahead, and you can't have that, so you have to go back and do something to their cabin to get back ahead, and now you're ahead. And they can't have that! So by the end of the week you've got neutron bombs going off on the side of the hills. One side tries to get ahead of the other.

I don't know how hardwired the need for revenge is in the species—maybe more hardwired into men than women—but God saw fit even in the Old Testament to address this problem.

So Jesus says, "You have heard that it was said, 'an eye for an eye and a tooth for a tooth.'" There's a technical term for that. It's called *lex talionis*. *Lex talionis* means, "An eye for an eye, a tooth for a tooth," and it sounds vicious, but what it actually intended to do was to place limits on the vengeance that one could take. So if I slammed your finger in a car door, you certainly have the right to slam my finger in the car door, but you don't have the right to put my head in there. That puts you ahead. You can only respond in kind, and so the basic principle to place limits on vengeance keeps it from escalating—so you don't have neutron bombs going off on the side of the hill.

But Jesus takes this principle and goes another place with it entirely. He says, "Not only do I not want you to over respond; I don't want you to respond with vengeance at all! "And he gives a series of really remarkable examples. "If anybody strikes you on the right cheek, then you turn the other cheek also and if anybody makes you carry their stuff for a mile, you offer to go another mile, and if anybody sues you and starts to take away your coat, you just give them all your clothes."

My reaction to that is probably the same as yours: "Have you lost your mind, Jesus! You really think this is going to work?" Several writers have pointed out that there does seem to be something humorous about this. So you strike me on the right cheek—and we are probably talking about the blow of insult here, not the blow of injury—and I turn my left cheek to you. What does that mean? Is Jesus asking us to invite another blow? Yes. So if you insult me, my proper response is an almost playful, "Is that all you got?" It does sound like Jesus is giving us a holy way to be a little bit lovingly sarcastic, to say, "Is that the best insult you've got? Surely given who I am you can do better than that."

And if a Roman soldier who had the power to make you grab his equipment—which was pretty heavy, by the way—and make you carry it a mile, then what you would typically do as a Jewish person in occupied territory once you did that mile would be to drop his pack and say, "Okay, I've done the amount required by law." But Jesus says what you do is turn to that guy and say, "You know it's only been a mile and I'm feeling strong. I would just love to carry your stuff another mile. It has been such an honor and a privilege to carry your stuff. This has just been the highlight of my day. Couldn't I carry it another mile for you?"

Or if somebody sues you and takes away your coat, say something like the following: "Well, as long as you're taking stuff, why don't you take all my clothes?" Of course, at some point this would get a little embarrassing.

It's as if Jesus is offering a holy pranksterism to counter violence and aggression. And before we dismiss Jesus' way too quickly, I just want to point out the way we've been doing it hasn't been working all that well. When you respond to violence with violence or to insult with insult, you don't get ahead. Nobody gets ahead and the world falls apart. So Jesus says don't get even; stop vengeance in its tracks by this winsome and humorous response that says if you want to get after me, you're going to have to do a lot better than that.

And then as he comes to the conclusion of the sermon he offers us the most difficult thing of all: "You've heard that it was said, 'You shall love your neighbors and hate your enemies.'" Now you might have a little trouble finding that verse in the

Old Testament, but you get the idea. You love the people of your tribe. You love the people of your cast. You love the people of your family.

Jesus was not saying the Old Testament teaches that you hate your enemies, but this is how people through the ages had lived and interpreted the law. Love those who are like you, but hate those who are different and keep your distance. But Jesus is going to give another way.

Jesus says when you love like that—loving only those who love you and hating your enemies—that makes you exactly like every pagan in the world, because everybody loves their own kind. Everybody loves people who respond to them in helpful and friendly ways. Everybody loves the members of their own tribe. What sets Christians apart is that we love people who aren't part of our tribe. We love people who treat us badly and maybe even violently. We love our enemies.

Does Jesus really mean this? Is it really possible to say, "I'm going to respond to my enemies, not with violence, but with redeeming love"?

You may be like me. You may be a little short of hard-core enemies. I'm sure I've got some, but I don't have very many. You have to have more personality that I have to have enemies. I just don't do the sort of things that you have to do to make enemies. I do have people who aren't members of my tribe, who aren't members of my family, who are to me outsiders. Am I going to love them?

The biggest challenge in my life is not loving my enemies. I have very few enemies. No, my biggest challenge is loving the irritants that God has placed in my life, because I may be a little short on enemies, but I'm chock full of irritants. The primary definition of irritants is that irritants do not know how irritating they are.

Okay, everybody has somebody in mind. Don't start laughing and poke the person beside you at this point then say what you are reading—he or she might get nervous!

Whenever I think of an irritant I think of a former student of mine named John. John was the most socially inept student I have ever had in twenty years of teaching. When I would see John coming towards my office, I would crawl under my desk and turn out the light just not to have to talk to him. John was totally inept and he had absolutely no idea the impact he had on other people.

I'm going to tell you one John story. You'll understand John perfectly. I had him in a small class later in the afternoon. There were only twelve people in the class. They're resentful about being there. They say, "Hey there's a baseball game on today!"

They know I like baseball.

"Will you let us go so we can go watch the game?"

"No, I can't do that," I said. "I have this class another time during the day and I have to keep the classes together. It's a teacher thing."

So they ask, "How fast could you give us the notes if we didn't interrupt you?"

I said I could do it in twenty minutes, and they said let's go for it, so we got this class project going.

I'm teaching Old Testament theology. Complicated stuff, so I go to the white board and start writing as fast as I can, and as I'm writing I turn around to make sure everything's good and my friend John on the front row has his hand up.

"Yes, John?"

John says, "I didn't get that back there. Could you go over that again?"

And so I go back to the board and I start to lecture again and I turn around and John's got his hand up.

I said, "Yes . . . John?"

John says, "You're going too fast, can you slow down a little bit? "

Now, I know we're in trouble. I turn around again and I start to write again, then I turn around and John's hand is up—again!

Now every ordinary person—if they weren't an irritant—would notice what is going on every time they put their hand up. John should have noticed that whenever he put his hand up everybody else in the room slapped their foreheads and said, "Oooooopppph!"

But John doesn't notice this because he's an irritant. So I'm back writing again and John's hand is up again. This time guns and knives appear all around the room, but John is oblivious. So I go back and start writing again and for the next fifteen minutes I lecture with my back to the class. I never turn back around. Now I know that was rude, but I saved John's life and that seemed more important at the time.

We all know a John, an irritant. We had a few students, our most mature students, who befriended John because they believed that you just don't love people who love you back, you love people even who are incapable of love or friendship, whether they're your enemies or irritants.

Jesus says when you love those who can't return your love, you change the world. Now that's a really good idea.

As I think about Jesus' words about violence and loving enemies, I get this picture in my mind of two cowboys, both with their guns pulled pointing them at each other. Each one is afraid to lower his weapon for fear that the other one will kill him. Switch the names and places and exchange guns for fists or knives and this has been the human experience worldwide almost from the beginning.

We believe that the only way to protect ourselves from violence is by being more violent. The only way to protect ourselves from our enemies is having more power than they have. And that's led our world to the brink of disaster because we have this ever escalating war of power and violence. It's hardly protected us. It's brought us to the brink of oblivion.

Jesus offers us another way. He says that when a person does something against us we don't retaliate at all and that we love our enemies rather than making war against them. Of all the teachings in the Sermon on the Mount, this is the one we believe the least and practice the least. We just don't believe that creative non-violence and love will overcome the powers of darkness in our world. And this is not about politics. How can we expect things to be different on a national or international level when we haven't begun to practice this peacemaking in our own lives?

We're too quick to retaliate. We're too quick to love only those of our tribe and see everyone else as a threat. Until this love of enemies becomes the way of our personal lives, we cannot expect it will be the way of national or international politics. To be a follower of Jesus means to love what he loves and hate what he hates, and it should be clear that what he hates is the violence and the conflict and the hatred in our world; but what he loves are the people who are on all sides of it. He says God sends his rain on the just and the unjust. This may be as big a challenge as we have anywhere in this field manual.

Are we going to be brave enough to be the cowboy who lowers our weapon? Will we be the cowgirl who says I'm tired of violence, I'm tired of retaliation, I'm tired of hatred. I want to try Jesus' way, the love of enemies.

Discussing What Jesus Says
Read Matthew 5:38–48

Jesus offers us another way. When someone does something against us, we don't retaliate. We love our enemies rather than making war on them. Of all the teachings on the Sermon on the Mount, we believe this the least. This is not about politics. No, until this love of enemies becomes the way of our personal lives, how can we expect politics to do this?

Does the legal system really keep us from being evil?

Can you hear some sarcasm in what Jesus is saying about turning the other cheek?

What if Jesus is offering a way to be holy pranksters?

Does responding to violence with violence work in our world today?

Do you have enemies?

How difficult it is to love "irritants"?

Are you willing to try Jesus' way, the love of enemies?

Doing What Jesus Says

The heart of this challenge is a belief in the power of Christ's love to transform a situation.

Anytime you recognize that you feel offended, coerced, or taken advantage of, immediately seek to bless the life of the person responsible.

1. Pray for God's eyes to see that person.

2. Plan something *very practical* (and imaginative, and silly, and fun) to show love to that person.
3. Here's the fun part: Put one hand in your back pocket (except when you're driving) until you have blessed them in some way or have a firm and exciting plan in place to do so.
4. Don't do this part way. Go over the top, and watch the radical love of God change the situation, or at least your heart!

Give to everyone who asks, and don't turn away from the one who wants to borrow from you. Seriously. Do it. Exactly what it says. That means the homeless guy pan-handling in the grocery store parking lot. That means the person at work or at school who wants to be friends but you never have time. That means (fill in the name of your worst irritant here). Obey this teaching as literally as possible for the next two weeks.

Chapter Nine

WATCH ME!
Matthew 6:1–18

Be careful not to practice your righteousness in front of others to be seen by them. If you do, you will have no reward from your Father in heaven.

So when you give to the needy, do not announce it with trumpets, as the hypocrites do in the synagogues and on the streets, to be honored by others. Truly I tell you, they have received their reward in full. But when you give to the needy, do not let your left hand know what your right hand is doing, so that your giving may be in secret. Then your Father, who sees what is done in secret, will reward you.

And when you pray, do not be like the hypocrites, for they love to pray standing in the synagogues and on the street corners to be seen by others. Truly I tell you, they have received their reward in full. But when you pray, go into your room, close the door and pray to your Father, who is unseen. Then your Father, who sees what is done in secret, will reward you. And when you pray, do not keep on babbling like pagans, for they think they will be heard because of their many words. Do not be like them, for your Father knows what you need before you ask him.

This, then, is how you should pray:

> *'Our Father in heaven,*
> *hallowed be your name,*
> *your kingdom come,*
> *your will be done,*
> > *on earth as it is in heaven.*
> *Give us today our daily bread.*
> *And forgive us our debts,*
> > *as we also have forgiven our debtors.*
> *And lead us not into temptation,*
> > *but deliver us from the evil one.'*

For if you forgive other people when they sin against you, your heavenly Father will also forgive you. But if you do not forgive others their sins, your Father will not forgive your sins.

When you fast, do not look somber as the hypocrites do, for they disfigure their faces to show others they are fasting. Truly I tell you, they have received their reward in full. But when you fast, put oil on your head and wash your face, so that it will not be obvious to others that you are fasting, but only to your Father, who is unseen; and your Father, who sees what is done in secret, will reward you.

What's one of the first things children say as soon as they can talk?

Watch me!

Even before children can talk, they want to be noticed, but when the ability to form words comes, the question they most want to ask is, "Can you see me?"

They want to know if you are watching. Mommy, did you see me do that somersault? Daddy, are you watching me run fast?

Those tricks they learn to perform aren't nearly as much fun if nobody's watching. Even as we grow older, we often don't grow out of the need to perform for the eyes of others. Because those tricks we perform are not nearly as much fun when nobody's watching.

No, adults aren't immune to doing things just because someone is watching. Someone said character is who you are when no one's watching. So what does it say about our character if we're obsessed with people watching what we do?

While shooting the video for this book, our production team and I visited a magnificent ballroom in the Abilene, Texas area. Walking through the cavernous ballroom with wooden floors, mirrors on the walls, vaulted ceilings, and chandeliers got me wondering how many parties had been thrown here for little other than to impress certain people—because when I throw my party I want to make sure you're watching. I want to make sure you're impressed.

Can you see me?

Jesus tells us that religious people aren't immune either. They are not immune to performing just so people will see them and be impressed. If I'm going to pray, I wonder who might happen by my office to see me. Will they be impressed? Can you see me?

Or if I'm going to give money, I wonder who is going to find out. Will they know I'm generous or think me a tightwad? Can you see me? Are you impressed?

If I fast, I wonder who will find out that I'm skipping meals? After a day or two of fasting, I'm impressed that I can do this, but I wonder who else is impressed. Are you watching? Are you impressed?

I want to make sure you're noticing what I'm doing, that you're watching and you're impressed.

Wanting to be seen seems to be a deeply ingrained human desire. Jesus knows this. Further, Jesus knows that this desire is a genuine threat to our spiritual lives. Why? Because I may be trying harder to impress you than I am to be in a relationship with God. Jesus tells us that God is watching but I might be more preoccupied with whether you're watching or not. Do you see me? Are you looking? Are you impressed?

I was working on a huge church program—I won't tell you what it was because some of you would recognize it. I was having to work with one particularly difficult, very famous Christian leader. He was somebody I had admired from afar, but when you got up close things didn't look quite as good. He was cranky. He was difficult. He was a prima donna, and he was very un-Jesus-like in his dealings with us. I was getting increasingly frustrated, and my friend who was helping me do this who's mostly a pagan said, "DDDW."

I said, "What does that mean?"

My friend said, "Haven't you ever been to a bar?"

"You're the expert on that. Tell me about it."

He says, "Well, you're in a bar and it's smoky and it's dark and you see somebody across the room. Got it?"

"Uh, yep. I am single and so far plan to stay that way, but that's beside the point."

"Right, but let's say you're interested in this woman, and you go over and you meet her."

"I wouldn't do that."

"Stick with me, okay? When you come back, you tell your friends, 'DDDW: Darkness and Distance Does Wonders!'"

When you get up close, most of us do not look nearly as good. All of us project an image of ourselves that we want people to see. Maybe we're hardwired for this. It seems deeply written into the DNA of humanity: I can't help but care what you think about me. So when I do my religious practices, I want God to be pleased, but I'd *really* be happy if *you* noticed, too.

I want you to know that I have quite an extraordinary prayer life. I've written a book to try to prove it! Have you noticed how much I pray? When I fast it's important that you know I'm fasting, because so few people fast, and this is a spiritual discipline for spiritual gurus. If I'm doing a seven-day fast, I not only want credit from God, I want credit from you for doing that. And I am an extraordinarily generous person, but it's amazing how much better I feel about my generosity if you know all about it. I gave this money away, and it was really sacrificial giving on my part—so, aren't you impressed?

Sure, none of us would put it that crassly. And most of us just aren't single minded about that, but we want people to notice.

Jesus says you have to be really careful about this stuff. He says when you do those sort of things to impress other people and they *are* impressed, congratulations. You got what you were looking for. But the one person who you were really trying to impress—God—isn't.

Why is God not impressed when we perform for the sake of impressing other people? Because God sees into the heart, who you really are. And God wants you to fast. He wants you to pray. He wants you to give your money away—but he doesn't want you to do all those things to impress other people. He wants you to do that out of your love and devotion for him. And those are two completely different things.

It's really interesting when you take in the Sermon on the Mount from beginning to end. You start to notice things that don't seem to add up. In Matthew 5 Jesus says, "Let your light so shine before men that they may see your good works and glorify your father who is in heaven." Got it? But then in Matthew 6, Jesus says never mind what I said about shining before people. Instead, he says to do what you do in secrecy so people don't know you're doing it.

How do we deal with this apparent contradiction?

Yes, there appears to be a contradiction, but I don't think there is one. In the first passage, he just wants you to live your life out in the public arena. He wants you to live your Christian life so people can see it and will glorify your Father, but in this second section we're doing what we do not to bear witness to the glory of God, but so that someone will be impressed with us. Those are completely different worlds. And so Jesus says, "Okay, let me give you a spiritual discipline that most people don't talk very much about: the discipline of secrecy."

When we use the word secrecy, it's almost always in a negative context. I've got a secret. Government secrets. Secret conspiracy. But Jesus says let me give you the positive side of secrecy. When you pray and fast and give your money away and do it so quietly, so secretly, that nobody knows, that is the best way to purify your motives. Because that way you know you're not doing it to impress other people. It's not foolproof. But it's a really good idea.

At a little church where I preached long ago, the discipline of secrecy somehow took hold; members of this church right and left were giving money away, praying and fasting and doing good works for others, and they did it in such secret ways that none of us could figure out who was doing what. And it became contagious. You just had this outbreak of secret goodness going on. And nobody was impressed with anybody else. We just said, "Praise God." And God who sees in secret rewards openly.

Jesus has this way of catching us. He goes right to the heart of our vulnerability here—this wanting to impress other people with our piety. He says careful, careful, do it in secret, but you have to cut this desire to impress other people out at the roots. Remember that you're working with an audience of one, and when you do things to impress other people this One is not impressed.

Jesus says secrecy is crucial to our spiritual lives because who we are when people aren't watching is who we really are. So as long as I'm doing my religious acts in front of people there's always this little part of me that hopes they're impressed, that hopes they're watching; so Jesus says, do it in the dark, do it in the closet, do it in secrecy because this is not about impressing other people.

Living the Jesus life is about loving God and being loved by God. We have to work hard at killing that desire to be seen, to be noticed, to impress people. God sees, but sometimes I'm more preoccupied with whether you see.

Righteous acts are not about being seen by people but about establishing a close relationship with God, and spiritual disciplines are the counterweight to the desire to do deeds to be seen by people.

Can you see me? Are you watching? Are you impressed?

Discussing What Jesus Says
Read Matthew 6:1–18

One of the greatest temptations of all time is to do good things for the wrong reasons, seeking affirmation from other human beings instead of from God. What if we lived our lives with an audience of One?

What is the counterweight Jesus proposes to the desire to impress other people?

What examples can you think of when you wanted human affirmation more than God's affirmation?

How do we break free from an addiction to affirmation from people that overshadows affirmation from God?

How do you view generosity? As something done in secret or done very publicly?

What do you think about secret generosity as a new spiritual discipline? How can you practice it?

Doing What Jesus Says

Learn a new discipline of secrecy. Please the One not the many.
  Look to do good deeds for people without them knowing it.
  Ask yourself when you do something good, "Am I doing this because it pleases God or others or myself?"

Chapter Ten

TREASURES IN HEAVEN
Matthew 6:19–24

Do not store up for yourselves treasures on earth, where moths and vermin destroy, and where thieves break in and steal. But store up for yourselves treasures in heaven, where moths and vermin do not destroy, and where thieves do not break in and steal. For where your treasure is, there your heart will be also.

The eye is the lamp of the body. If your eyes are healthy, your whole body will be full of light. But if your eyes are unhealthy, your whole body will be full of darkness. If then the light within you is darkness, how great is that darkness!

No one can serve two masters. Either you will hate the one and love the other, or you will be devoted to the one and despise the other. You cannot serve both God and money.

I am a great admirer of a group of young adults who live in community together. They call it the Allelon Community. Allelon is a Greek word meaning "one another."

The house for Allelon Community is in one of the forgotten neighborhoods of Abilene, Texas, where the poorest people in the city live. One day I visited with three members of the community who live in the house. Their names are Wes, Aaron, and Kyle. These three and others in Allelon Community live a very simple life. Because they live in one of the worst neighborhoods in Abilene and have chosen to live this life, I think they can tell us some things about Jesus' instructions about materialism and worry.

The first part of this chapter will be an interview with the Allelon Community. In the very unified style of Allelon, I will simply show "Allelon" as the "one" responding to my questions, though Wes, Aaron, and Kyle each gave answers.

Randy: You are very generous with your money and with your time. Don't you ever get concerned about whether you're going to be taken care of? You share everything. You give things away. People are constantly running through your house. How do you take care of yourselves?

Allelon: Yes. Sometimes I get worried about myself. You know what Jesus says in the Sermon on the Mount about worry and stuff is possibly one of the hardest sections in the sermon. Even though I know that God is a Father who loves to give good gifts to his children and that he takes care of the lilies and sparrows, still, a lot of times I do get worried. But that's why we've tried to make intentional moves to organize our lives in such a way that we build in accountability. On those days when it is hard to believe in God as provider or to trust in God, we made some intentional decisions to set our lives up in a way that, whether or not I'm feeling it in my heart right now, my lifestyle is an act of faith in God as provider.

Randy: Do you feel as if you're depriving yourselves? Does it feel sacrificial? Most people, if they lived the life you are living, would think, *Oh boy, all the sacrifices I've made for Jesus . . . . I can't believe what I've had to give up for Jesus.* Is that what it feels like?

Allelon: Not for me. I was explaining to somebody just the other day that I don't know how I would function if I were on my own and having to come up with a higher rent that was just for me, rather than sharing a rent payment and utility payment. The sacrifice for me would be having to work a job that I hate. But instead, because we share everything in common, I'm freer to pursue my passions, even in work.

Randy: When I've talked about you guys to other people, I say what's really interesting is I've never seen you more alive or happier than since you've been doing this.

Allelon: I think a lot of it stems out of the idea of community. We help take care of each other. When you don't have to take care of yourself you're free to be yourself and so you can be happier with things you want to do. Before, when I was working all the time trying to just make sure I was getting things taken care of, I was just miserable at a job I didn't really enjoy. When other people are looking out for your needs, you don't have to look out for yourself alone.

Randy: Jesus says you can't serve two masters—you can't serve God and material things. He says not to worry but to seek the kingdom first. Do you just think that's highfalutin language? Do you actually think that's a life you can live?

Allelon: Yes. It's possible, but for me it has not been an instant choice. I mean it's an almost day-by-day thing where I'm seeking to live more fully into this. Once you start really sinking your teeth into the fruit of putting other people higher, at least with your schedules, putting other people ahead of your time, then it just . . . it's addictive.

Randy: Most people aren't going to make the fairly radical moves that you've made. If you can tell them one thing about this passage of Scripture that they need to hear that would make a difference in their lives, what would you want to say to them about your experience?

Allelon: Well, one thing I would say is if you are trying to simplify and learn to trust God just because you know Matthew 6 has some really beautiful words about it, it probably won't happen. I mean, if you're doing it because it's a really cool thing to do, it probably won't happen. For me, that's why it's so important to understand that God is trustworthy and that he provides; it's rooted in love which is right at the very heart of God.

To me it comes back to the great commandment. Love God and love your neighbors. And If we want to love our neighbors, it's not hard to see what that requires; but we're only able to do that when we understand what's going on in Matthew 6, that God really can be trusted to provide, that when we seek first his kingdom, all these things really will be added because that's part of God's nature for those who love him and love their neighbors. I hope the people who are looking into this can think about some little moves they can make towards the worry-free life, a life that trusts God.

The Allelon community has taught me much about trusting God. Here are my further thoughts on this passage.

If you made a list of every topic that Jesus addressed and you determined their importance by how many times Jesus talked about each one, money would be very near the top of the list.

Generally we get really uncomfortable when we start talking about money because who's going to pass judgment on the proper lifestyle for a Christian in twenty first century America? But Jesus is different. Maybe it's because he's the Son of God, but he doesn't have any qualms about that. He just barges in and says, "Okay, I'm going to talk to you about the way you live." He says it all has to do with your eyes. He says if your eyes are good, your whole body is full of light, and if your eyes are bad, your whole body is full of darkness. He's playing on this term "evil eye" and this evil eye is an eye of covetousness.

When your eye always looks to covet, he says it makes you full of darkness. We've got to think about what it's like to live in a culture that is built around coveting. We have whole industries in America whose sole job is to make you covet. Their task is to make you want things that you don't have, and if they're really good at it, they make you want things you don't even need. Their job is to convince you that if you've got an iPhone you've got to have the next edition. And if you've got a computer, the one you have is not good enough. You've got to have the latest and the best. And they are really, really good at what they do. I'm amazed at what I find myself wanting that I never knew existed a few minutes before.

How do we have good eyes in this culture? Jesus says, I want to be clear about this. Nobody can serve two masters. You're either going to love one and hate the other and cling to one and reject the other. He says you can't serve both God and money.

I like stuff but I'm serving God, so I'm not going to serve money. But then Jesus says, "Okay, let me give you a little test." And there's this test right in the text. This is the way the test goes: wherever your treasure is, there will your heart be.

Now this is one of those passages where we have built-in dyslexia. When we read the text, we immediately flip it in our minds. We say to ourselves that this is what the text says: "Wherever your heart is, that's where your money will be—your treasure."

But that's not what Jesus says. Jesus says, "Wherever your treasure is, that's where your heart is."

It's a test. Do you want to know what you're serving? Do you want to know what you're investing in? Then look at where you put your time. Where do you put your money? That's who your master is.

Let me give you an example that has nothing to do with money. Years ago in a place far away I helped convert a young man. He and his wife had not been married very long. They were having problems in their marriage and, of all things, he came to me for help in his marriage. That's how desperate he was. I was the only real Christian he knew. So I hadn't had time to disciple him. He was a very new Christian.

So I said to the guy, "Okay, do you want to save your marriage?"

"Absolutely."

"How much?" I asked.

"It's the most important thing in the world to me."

"Then we have a chance," I said. "Tell me about your life."

"Life is really good. Business is booming, and I'm moving up the ladder. I love sports and spend a lot of time playing sports with my friends," he said.

Indeed, he was a superb intercollegiate athlete; he held several records that may still be in the books for all I know. So he liked to play sports with the guys and the plain fact of the matter is he was pretty invested in all parts of his life—but, he was giving very little to his marriage.

So, given my very direct approach to marriage counseling, I said, "Okay, I think I see the problem. Here's the problem. Either you're a liar or Jesus is because Jesus says wherever your treasure is—wherever your investment is—that's where your heart is. So you tell me your heart is in saving your marriage, but all of your treasure's going someplace else."

The challenge was issued and the man had to decide for himself whether he was going to go back and invest in what he said was most important to him. He was investing in everything else except what he said was his treasure.

Well, we need to take the test. How much time do we spend thinking about stuff? How much investment do we have cleaning our stuff? Protecting our stuff? Upgrading our stuff? I often think that when Jesus calls those apostles and says come and follow me, I'd say, "Okay, I'd be happy to, but it's going to take me a while, because I have to get everything in order since I've got so much stuff. There are a lot of things I need to take care of."

Then Jesus says, "Where's your investment? Where's your time? Where's your money?"

And then as you come to the end of the chapter, he gives you the key. He says, "This is what I want you Christians to do. When it comes to material stuff, I want you to stop worrying."

Oh. Stop worrying. That was easy. That's a lot like telling somebody in Houston in summer to quit sweating. It's not like I can just decide one day to stop worrying about stuff anymore. I'm a lot like you.

A couple of years ago when the economy crashed all my investments crashed too. My money manager calls me up and says, "I guess you've seen what happened to your investments?"

"Yes, as a matter of fact, I have."

"I wanted to make sure you weren't getting ready to jump off a bridge," she said.

"I live in Abilene, Texas. That's a bad choice. This is Texas. I should be thinking about shooting myself. Guns are cheap and plentiful here," I said.

I'm not sure she knew how to respond to my attempt at humor. So I went on to say, "You and I don't know each other well enough. I haven't thought about suicide a single time," I said.

"That's good," she said, sounding relieved.

But I added, "Now, I have been thinking about homicide almost continually. So you need to stay on your side of town until you have different news to deliver!"

And in those moments we find out how we're wired. How anxious does it make you? Are you worried about it? And Jesus says, here is the key: You have to believe in the provision of God.

He paints several word pictures from nature. Look how God takes care of the birds. Look how God clothes the grass of the field. And if God does that for birds and grass, don't you think he's going to take care of you? And I think our truthful response to that is, "I'm not sure."

When we really believe in the provision of God, it allows us to be generous in whole new ways because we know God's got us. And when I'm anxious and worried and tight-fisted with my stuff, it's because I'm just not sure about God. I've got to take care of myself because I don't know about God. I don't know if he'll come through. So Jesus says, "Believe me. God's got you. If he knows how to take care of the birds, he's got you, so quit worrying. Quit being obsessed with money. You seek the kingdom and God's got you."

I don't know about you, but to me that sounds like a much better way to live.

Most of us are not going to adopt the lifestyle of the Allelon Community, though what I hope you've heard is that Jesus' way is not only livable but makes life worth living. I hope you find the joy in life you've always looked for and learn that the things you thought were so important maybe aren't quite as important as you thought. Who wouldn't want to live a worry free life? Who wouldn't want to believe in the provision of God and find the rich life of community and sharing that Jesus invites us to?

Maybe you can find some small steps to make into that life. God will meet you there.

Discussing What Jesus Says
Read Matthew 6:19–24

When many people on earth love things and use people, having our treasure in heaven means using things and loving people.

Could you live in or even visit a bad neighborhood in your town?

Would you rather have a job you hate and keep all the money for yourself, or have a fulfilling job and share the salary with family and friends?

Do you feel as if you need to take care of yourself because you're not sure God will?

Do we really believe God can be trusted to provide for you?

What is the time and investment you have in stuff compared to how much time and investment you have in relationships with God and others?

Do you love things and use people or love people and use things?

Doing What Jesus Says

In his classic book, *Celebration of Discipline,* Richard J. Foster lists ten biblical principles for living out inward simplicity in outward ways. He cautions turning these into legalism.

> "Buy things for their usefulness and not their status."
> "Reject anything that is producing an addiction in you."
> "Develop a habit of giving things away."
> "Refuse to be propagandized by the custodians of modern gadgetry."
> "Learn to enjoy things without owning them."
> "Develop a deeper appreciation for the creation."
> "Look with a healthy skepticism at all 'buy now, pay later' schemes."
> "Obey Jesus' instructions about plain, honest speech."
> "Reject anything that breeds the oppression of others."
> "Shun anything that distracts you from seeking first the kingdom of God."

Chapter Eleven

STICK IN MY EYE
Matthew 7:1–14

Do not judge, or you too will be judged. For in the same way you judge others, you will be judged, and with the measure you use, it will be measured to you.

Why do you look at the speck of sawdust in your brother's eye and pay no attention to the plank in your own eye? How can you say to your brother, 'Let me take the speck out of your eye,' when all the time there is a plank in your own eye? You hypocrite, first take the plank out of your own eye, and then you will see clearly to remove the speck from your brother's eye.

Do not give dogs what is sacred; do not throw your pearls to pigs. If you do, they may trample them under their feet, and turn and tear you to pieces.

Ask and it will be given to you; seek and you will find; knock and the door will be opened to you. For everyone who asks receives; the one who seeks finds; and to the one who knocks, the door will be opened.

Which of you, if your son asks for bread, will give him a stone? Or if he asks for a fish, will give him a snake? If you, then, though you are evil, know how to give good gifts to your children, how much more will your Father in heaven give good gifts to those who ask him! So in everything, do to others what you would have them do to you, for this sums up the Law and the Prophets.

Enter through the narrow gate. For wide is the gate and broad is the road that leads to destruction, and many enter through it. But small is the gate and narrow the road that leads to life, and only a few find it.

Whenever you hear the statement, "She's a generous person!" we're almost always talking about money. She's willing to give and to give a lot.

In Matthew 7, however, Jesus gives us a completely different way to think about generosity. He talks about generosity in our judgments of other people.

What would happen if we developed such generosity of spirit? Jesus grounds this generosity in the nature of God himself. Rather than depending on the government to take care of you, count on God to give you the good gifts that you need. Then the generosity of God can become your generosity.

Maybe we don't believe in God's generosity, but once we come to understand how gracious he's been to us, it ought to empower us to have that same sort of graciousness towards other people. Don't judge me! That's the one thing people say over and over. They don't want to be judged. They don't want you to pass judgment on their lifestyle.

We frequently hear that Christians are too judgmental. Well, Jesus doesn't totally prohibit making judgments here. You can't get through life without making judgments. What he does do is suggest that we need to be as generous in our judgments as we want generosity to be given to us—and we need to be as generous in our judgments as God is. I wonder what would happen if generosity had to do, not with just how much money we gave, but with the respect we gave to other people. If we came to believe that every person was worthy of respect just as we want to be respected. The world might look a little different if we were a little slower to judge and a little quicker to practice the Golden Rule: to treat other people the way we want to be treated.

There's not a lot of obvious humor in the Sermon on the Mount. The one section that Jesus seems to play for laughs is the beginning of chapter 7 where he talks about our propensity to judge others more harshly that we judge ourselves. It's now a famous passage where he says, "Okay, how are you going to take a speck out of your brother's eye when you've got this beam in your own eye. First take the beam out of your eye so you can see to take the speck out of your brother's eye." It's a humorous picture of this person with a log in his eye trying to do fine surgery on somebody else's eye. It hits us where we live because judgmentalism is a way of life with us.

I can be particularly judgmental in those areas of life where I have my act together. And so when I have my act together in a certain area and you don't, it is really easy for me to be judgmental about it. And the only areas I'm ever going to focus on are the ones where I'm far superior to you anyway. If we get into some area where your life may be a little better, I'm will quickly change the subject until we get to that area where my life is in better shape so that I can look down on yours. We don't like to admit it, but we do it all the time.

Jesus here isn't telling us that you can't make any sort of judgments at all. In fact, in the Sermon on the Mount, especially towards the end of chapter 7, he insists that you need to make some judgments about who truly speaks for Jesus. But his point is to warn us that we have this tendency to judge too quickly, to judge unfairly, to push harsh judgments on other people.

One of my colleagues starts out by asking this simple question: "Who does monkey girl marry?" And the answer to the question is alligator man. And it's a true story. Monkey girl and alligator man were sideshow freaks, at least that's what you called them in the old days before political correctness. Monkey girl had long silken hair everywhere, including her face. Alligator man had reptilian skin. And believe it or not, they fell in love with each other. And it was quite the romance. I mean, it's really a sweet story in a Stephen King sort of way. And not only did they fall in love with each other, they got married. Apparently monkey girl's parents had some questions about it, thinking she was getting ready to marry beneath her. But anyway, they got it together. And then my colleague asks the really interesting question: I wonder what monkey girl and alligator man say to each other when they get into a knock down drag out fight. Do you think alligator man looks at her and says, "I can't believe I married a freak like you"? only to catch his own reflection in the mirror. And of course his point is this: we're all freaks of nature.

So this story of monkey girl and alligator man illustrates how one of the best ways for me to lose that judgmental spirit towards you is to take a long hard look at myself. And when I look at the ways that my life is wounded and out of shape, then I'm a little more generous towards you. Once I start to deal with my own stuff, then I can be a little more charitable towards yours.

I had a friend who used to have to sit through two chapels a day at a Christian university, and over a thirty year period he heard some of the worst chapel speeches in the history of the world—twice. And he taught me one of the most important principles I've ever learned: the benefit-of-the-doubt principle. He said when speakers said something that you could take more than one way, he always tried to give them the benefit of the doubt and take it in the best possible way. My whole life I'd been doing just the opposite. When a person said something you could take two possible ways, I always took it the worst possible way. What would the world look like if we gave the benefit of the doubt and took seriously our own freakish nature before we started to pass judgment on others?

And then there's the weirdest verse in the whole sermon. Jesus transitions and says, "Don't cast your pearls before swine. Don't give what is holy to dogs or they will turn on you and rip you to pieces." Many commentators have connected this verse with the verses on judgment. But I'm convinced it doesn't go with those verses. It goes with the ones that follow where Jesus says this: "Ask and it shall be given you. Seek and you shall find. Knock and the door shall be opened to you. Because even though you're evil, you know how to give good gifts; how much more will your father give good gifts to you." He says, Hey when your son comes to you and asks you for a fish, you're not going to give him a snake. In the same say, your Father will be generous in giving good gifts to you.

So what do those two ideas have to do with each other? Well, it's obvious that when Jesus talks about pigs and dogs, he's not talking about animals. He's talking about people. We're already uncomfortable. Don't call people pigs and dogs. But a typical Jew of ancient Israel would look at certain people as pigs and dogs—namely, Gentiles or non-Jews. And this is probably not just any Gentile, but a Roman occupier, and so in effect Jesus says in this passage, "Don't give what is sacred to the Roman occupying powers." That is, don't give your allegiance, don't give your support, don't give your assurance to the government.

So what is the alternative to finding assurance in and giving allegiance and support to our nation or the powers that be? Jesus says the alternative is to ask God, and he'll give you what you need. In other words, he calls upon us to believe in the generosity of God and find our security there rather than finding it in some governmental power. And then he says that when you do that, when you accept the generosity of God, then you can be generous to other people. You treat them the way you want to be treated.

Now the generosity of God becomes your generosity.

So what do these passages all have in common? If I can accept that God has been generous towards me when he could have been judgmental, when I accept the notion that God is going to give me the good gifts that I need, then that empowers me to be generous to other people in the way that God is generous to me. I no longer have to pass harsh judgments on you. I can give you the benefit of the doubt. And I no longer have to find my security in politics. I find my security in God.

As a result, I start to treat other people the way that God has treated me. God's generosity becomes my generosity and that changes the world. What would the world be like if we replaced insecure, judgmental, anxious people with people who are so confident in God's generosity that they don't have to pass judgment? Can you imagine what that world would look like? I don't know about you, but that sounds like a really good idea to me.

We see what we're looking for. If we're not looking for something, we often don't see it. In this passage Jesus asks us to change the way we look at people. If we're looking for what's worst in them, if we're looking for things to be judgmental about, they're pretty easy to find. But if we look at them with the same generosity that God looks at us, then we see a completely different picture.

Jesus teaches us to use generosity much differently than how we often use it in our culture. We use generosity in relation to someone's use of money. But Jesus uses the idea of generosity in a much different way. He talks about generosity in terms of judgment. Jesus teaches us that God's generosity of judgment is the foundation for our generosity of judgment. It's a generosity of love. It's a generosity of spirit. It's a generosity of giving the benefit of the doubt.

What would happen if God's generosity became our generosity? If, when we looked at other people, we looked, not for what was worse in them, but we looked for the image of God that's in every human being? What if we showed the same generosity to other people that we want them to show us when they look at us?

We all have woundedness and brokenness and things that we can be judgmental about, but we also have the image of God that's been placed in each one of us—and what we see is largely determined by what we're looking for. In this passage, Jesus doesn't give a complete prohibition against judging. You can't go through life without making judgments. He just tells us that when we judge, we ought to let God's generosity become our generosity, and not just a generosity of money, but a generosity of spirit. A generosity of judgment.

When Jesus says that we can trust God to give us good gifts, he presents his Father as the model of the one who knows how to take care of us, who will be generous with all that he has.

What if we were generous, not just with our money, but with all that we have? What if we were generous with our love, our sympathy, our compassion, our spirit? Then we would be able to live out in very practical ways Jesus' instruction, "Don't judge others except in ways that you want to be judged."

Discussing What Jesus Says

Read Matthew 7:1–14

When Jesus says that we can trust God to give us good gifts, he presents his Father as the model of the one who knows how to take care of us, who will be generous with all that he has. What if we were generous, not just with our money, but with all that we have? What if we were generous with our love, our sympathy, our compassion, our spirit? Then we would be able to live out in very practical ways Jesus' instruction, "Don't judge others except in ways that you want to be judged."

Are we not to judge at all or just not judge too harshly?

What would happen in relationships if everyone adopted the benefit-of-the-doubt principle?

Are you particularly judgmental in areas where you think you have your act together?

Do you change the subject when something comes up that you are not particularly good at?

Doing What Jesus Says

Speak only what love requires. What does that mean? Decide on a time period and experiment with speaking only out of love. That means no judgmental or harsh tone or talking.

The next part will be hard for some: no sarcastic speech. Speaking only what love requires means bringing focus to what you say, saying things that loving people requires but nothing more. It may require you to be more silent than normal.

Chapter Twelve

WOLVES IN SHEEP'S CLOTHING
Matthew 7:15–23

Watch out for false prophets. They come to you in sheep's clothing, but inwardly they are ferocious wolves. By their fruit you will recognize them. Do people pick grapes from thorn bushes, or figs from thistles? Likewise, every good tree bears good fruit, but a bad tree bears bad fruit. A good tree cannot bear bad fruit, and a bad tree cannot bear good fruit. Every tree that does not bear good fruit is cut down and thrown into the fire. Thus, by their fruit you will recognize them.

Not everyone who says to me, 'Lord, Lord,' will enter the kingdom of heaven, but only the one who does the will of my Father who is in heaven. Many will say to me on that day, 'Lord, Lord, did we not prophesy in your name and in your name drive out demons and in your name perform many miracles?' Then I will tell them plainly, 'I never knew you. Away from me, you evildoers!'

I teach Bible and theology at Abilene Christian University. Nearly every day I walk past a magnificent sculpture on campus called "Jacob's Dream." The artist worked on it for years. Most people have no idea how much of his life he poured into this. He shed gallons of sweat, blood, and tears over this project, and with the exception of his friends, nobody really cares about that. What most people are concerned about is the final result—how it turned out. In business, this is called the bottom line. In the Sermon on the Mount, Jesus calls this bottom line the fruit of a person's work.

The last major teaching section in the Sermon on the Mount is the most haunting and disconcerting piece in the whole sermon. Jesus talks about how he keeps score and it's a little bit scary.

It's not Jesus' talk about wolves that's scary to me. This section starts out with Jesus saying, "Beware of wolves in sheep's clothing." They look safe enough, but they're out to get you. And we all know there are plenty of hypocrites out there. This is not the part that scares me.

There are all sorts of people doing things in the name of Jesus Christ that don't represent Christ very well. There are people who are trying to assert power over other people. There are people out there trying to get money and they talk a good game, but they are nothing but ferocious wolves seeking to devour. And it is hard to overestimate how much damage such people have done to the cause of Christ. You can have a hundred Christians who represent Jesus well and you can have one of these people who can destroy the work of those hundred Christians. We've seen plenty of studies in the literature saying that people who are outside the Christian faith regard Christians as being hypocritical or two-faced. I suspect that a lot of television preachers have to bear a lot of the blame for that.

But this business of wolves in sheep's clothing is not the part of the passage that haunts me most. You certainly have to watch out for those folks. You need to expose them. But then the passage shifts focus to another group of people.

We all know that not everybody who claims to be from Christ is and not everything that is done in Christ's name really represents Christ. We've all known hypocrites who say one thing and do another and do it for bad reasons, either for gaining power over another person or money, and those hypocrites are bad for Christian faith and they're bad for the world. But the more haunting part of this passage is those people who are doing miracles and prophesying and casting out demons in Jesus' name, and Jesus says, "I never knew you."

There's this group of people that says, "But Jesus, didn't we prophesy in your name and didn't we do miracles and didn't we cast out demons?" And Jesus says to them, "I never knew you." I don't know if these are hypocrites or if these are people who really believe that they are serious followers of Jesus but who somehow they lost track of what Jesus thought was really important.

What haunts and scares me is that I would never want Jesus to say this to me. Would you? Imagine Jesus looking you in the eyes and saying, "I never knew you."

But Jesus tells us how to avoid such a response. And here is where Jesus moves to the way he keeps score.

He keeps score by using the image of fruit. I don't like horticultural images because I am no good with plants. We have a mutual relationship that can only be described as antagonistic.

I had a member of my family die and somebody gave me this plant, and I said, "You gave me a live plant? What is wrong with you?"

"Oh, there's absolutely NO way you can kill this plant."

"Ha! You don't know me very well!"

The plant didn't last long. If I go to the greenhouse section of a store, plants scream, "NO! Please, not me, don't take me! I'm too young to die."

So I don't really understand horticulture images, but I think I get this: Good trees bear good fruit. Bad trees bear bad fruit.

In other words, you don't plant quality seed and nurture a good lemon tree and reap withered lemons or a different fruit like apples off of the tree. I think I understand that image. So Jesus says you will know those "ferocious wolves" by their fruit. A good tree cannot bear bad fruit and a bad tree cannot bear good fruit.

I don't care for plants, but I do like sports. So see if this makes sense to you. Jesus is talking about how to keep score. How do we know what the score is in our lives? Jesus doesn't exactly keep score the way we do. I think that I would be impressed by casting out demons. If you did a miracle, I'd be super impressed. I like those. Prophecy? I would give you high marks—now that's running up the score! Sounds great to me.

More personally, Jesus, aren't you impressed by all the sermons I've preached? Aren't you impressed by all my prayers? Aren't you impressed by all the classes I've taught? And then Jesus says, "I'm not sure I know you." Because if I'm understanding the sermon right, Jesus is keeping score a totally different way. You look at a person's life and see how it measures up beside the Sermon on the Mount.

And how does your life compare to the teachings of Jesus in the Sermon on the Mount?

Could Jesus be challenging you in ways you've never been challenged before when you honestly compare your life to his teachings?

Could he be saying, "What I want for you is a life free of your stuff"? Or could he be saying, "What I really want for you is to be a person of integrity and honesty"? Or perhaps he's saying to you, "What I really wanted was for you to be someone who loves relentlessly." Is there fruit that Jesus wants in your life that you are not producing? Are you a good tree producing good fruit or a bad tree producing bad fruit?

I go to a lot of churches to preach, and occasionally I'll go to one that's sick. And when I go to a church that's really sick, it's almost always because somebody has been committing theological malpractice there. Because somebody has lost sight of what Jesus really thinks is important. And he says it's by the fruit you will know. And in this day and age when there are so many crazy things being said in the name of Jesus, we need to remind ourselves of this. When you follow Jesus Christ it will never lead you to hurt or abuse or marginalize any group of people; when that happens, that's not just bad living—that's a result of bad doctrine. True teaching doesn't do that. It loves. It embraces. It transforms. It never humiliates. It never abuses. It never puts down.

When you pass the half-century age mark, you start to look at your life and wonder how you've done. What does the scorecard look like? How are you keeping score in your life? Is it the same way that Jesus keeps score? How are you going to keep score?

In my life, I might look at how many classes or students I've taught. By contrast, I might keep score by whether or not the Sermon on the Mount is a little more present in the lives of the people around me than it was before. That's how Jesus keeps score. This last little teaching section in the Sermon on the Mount in some ways captures the essence and pulls it all together. It tells us, Okay, if you really want to know how you're doing, let me give you a score sheet. It's called the Sermon on the Mount and all you have to do is look and see if this is the fruit of your life. I don't know about you, but that sounds like a really good idea to me.

What if I spent my life doing things that weren't really as important to Jesus as they were to me? What if I said, "Jesus, I taught the Bible classes. I preached the sermons. I did all these good works in your name." And Jesus says, "I never really knew you. What I was interested in is you living a life free of materialism and full of integrity and love. What I wanted was a life lived according to the Sermon on the Mount."

The Sermon on the Mount is a full scorecard for life. It's the way Jesus keeps score. That's his bottom line. What if I spent my whole life caring about things that Jesus really didn't care that much about? When all he wanted was a life formed according to the cross. A cross-shaped life. A life lived according to the Sermon on the Mount.

Discussing What Jesus Says
Read Matthew 7:15–23

The Sermon on the Mount is a full score card for life. It's the way Jesus keeps score. That's his bottom line. What if you spent your whole life caring about things that Jesus really didn't care that much about? When all he wanted was a life formed according to the cross. A cross-shaped life. A life lived according to the Sermon on the Mount.

Have you ever done some big project and no one appreciated anything of your work except for the bottom line?

Jesus keeps score differently from the way we do. How do you keep score in your relationships?

How do you keep score with co-workers?

How does your church keep score with one another?

What are some practical ways you can change the way you keep score with one another in your home?

Doing What Jesus Says

Try to identify three things that are really important to Jesus in the Sermon on the Mount. Once you identify these three things, choose a period of one week to several weeks and try to live out of those things for that time period.

What does it mean to "live out" three important things? For example, one of the things that is really important to Jesus is loving our neighbor. What if you took loving your neighbor more seriously, even more literally? Have you ever talked to some of your neighbors who live next to you? Do you view your family members as neighbors whom you must love and treat right daily?

LIVING THE
SERMON

I want to tell you a story about how I came to agree with a group of young men to make a covenant to live out the Sermon on the Mount.

When I was in graduate school, I read Richard Foster's book, *Celebration of Discipline*. When that book came out, there was nothing else like it. There are plenty of books like that now, but at the time *Celebration of Discipline* hit me like a bolt of lightning out of the sky. I wondered, *Where has this stuff been all my life?*

I went on to do doctoral work at Syracuse University, and while I was there I was working with a church that was going through some really difficult times. I tried to help but generally made a mess of it. And during that time, I don't think I would have made it without the things I learned from Foster's book. Those disciplines that led me more deeply into relationship with God basically saved my life. I got to share that with Richard Foster a few years ago, and that was a great moment.

At same time, I was studying theology and philosophy, and increasingly I became interested in how the gospel reaches the darkest places in culture. But there was a problem. I had reasonable mastery of the biblical tradition, but very little understanding of the mystical and contemplative traditions.

Monasticism and the contemplative life had long seemed to be a Catholic or high church thing, but I continued to be interested and in 2001 I experienced a transformative event in my life. By "accident" I came across this monastery called the Lebh Shomea House of Prayer. The purpose of the house of prayer is to give a person a place to spend times of quiet prayer. And I wondered, *What would happen if I gave God my undivided attention for forty days?*

So I spent time there and this experience basically changed my life's mission and direction. I wanted to understand how someone can have a deep commitment to the contemplative life but also engage the world with the gospel story. So I set about learning from the mystical and contemplative traditions, but with a view toward also living a missional life. In my experience contemplatives didn't seem very missional and missional people didn't seem very contemplative. Was there a community that took both of these very seriously?

This led to spending time in a Celtic retreat house, and I learned from Trappist monks, went to an Ignatian retreat house, and even spent time learning about Buddhist meditation. I did a two-year program in the Shalem Institute, learning to do contemplative spiritual direction.

One of the places I found in my searching over a decade that was really committed to the contemplative life but also deeply committed to impacting the world was the Church of the Savior in Washington, D.C. They are really doing what Elaine Heath's *Mystic Way of Evangelism* calls us to do: bring together the contemplative and missional lives as a powerful way of following Jesus.

As a college professor, I'm very interested in spiritual formation, but college students are notoriously difficult to form. It's a great formative age, but many students have also checked out of church. So I began to wonder, *Is there a way to form that population that will permanently take?* They are probably never going to be able to replicate their four-year college experience, so what are the ways to form them that will impact them for the rest of their lives?

That question and the journey of finding contemplative and missional communities led me toward an experiment I'm doing now with students on the Abilene Christian University campus.

I had done a lot of mentoring of students, but it always seemed to be from the neck up. It wasn't bad and it impacted a lot of people, but I wanted to know if there was another level of engagement. So for a long time I had in the back of my mind setting up a religious order of college students who would be committed to following Jesus. A friend of mine told me that if you wait until you feel ready you're never going to do this, so you need to plunge in and make mistakes. That's what I've done.

I began studying some helpful books about religious orders and rules. We don't need to be afraid of the word "rule" or "religious order." A rule is simply a way of life that a group of people commit to live.

Two books especially helped me understand how to establish orders that are not bound by a monastery but where people are really living. I read *The New Friars* by Scott Bessenecker and *Punk Monk* by Andy Freeman and Pete Greig, who come out of the British 24/7 prayer movement and build on Benedictine disciplines.

So I began devising a plan to form of group of freshmen and develop a three and a half year plan, taking in a new group every year and having the upperclassmen continue on in the group.

The basic commitment of the group is living out the Sermon on the Mount together. We would all sign a covenant to live basic principles of the teachings of Christ like loving neighbors, practicing deep integrity, and sexual purity. One of the things that has surprised me—I should have known—is how signing on to a covenant is truly powerful. They sign up to a basic rule, and something about signing that and committing to it is very powerful. They've taken their vows seriously. They haven't lived them perfectly but seriously.

The young men also covenant to hold each other graciously accountable. What does that mean? They give others in the group permission to speak into each other's lives. If someone sees you on the soccer field not representing Jesus well, what do you want them to say to you? They've given permission to speak into each other's lives. We've prayed very specifically about sin in our lives.

We have some rituals that identify us, including chanting prayers. Part of our rule is that we memorize the Sermon on the Mount. The old guys had it right that when we memorize Scripture, it gets into you in ways it doesn't when you just read it.

People often balk at memorizing, thinking they can't do it, but everyone has capacity to memorize; we have this store of songs in our heads at all times, even get songs stuck in our heads. Memorizing Scripture can access that same part of the brain, particularly when chanted or sung or prayed. To keep it fresh in memory, I have to dust it off, have to go back and review. It doesn't take as long as most people think it does to memorize, but it does take intentional work.

It would radically change our churches if all our church leaders took time to memorize the Sermon on the Mount. When you are doing it, you're not doing anything bad. And I believe it would have a great formational impact on the church.

When we get together, we also do exercises and challenges together. One of our exercises at meals is that you cannot serve yourself or ask to be served. So how do we eat? We watch and see if others need something, a drink or a plate of food; so we have to look around and notice people's needs and fill them for one another.

We do a lot of dwelling in the Word. This means that we read a section from the Sermon on the Mount then talk in groups and ask questions like this: If we took this teaching about loving our enemies seriously, what would we do? So in our meetings we frequently formulate what we call challenges or experiments to go out and live this out. These are the challenges that have been issued at the end of each of the chapters in this book. When we keep piling these challenges or experiments up, a sort of critical mass develops and we become different people.

The accountability to and expectations for one another is producing good results—and more quickly than I imagined. Guys who were struggling with their spiritual lives have more confidence and the relationships are pretty dynamic. I think they would tell you it's made a huge difference in their lives. It's a three and a half year process, but the payoff is ten years down the road. This is probably not something they will ever be able to repeat in a college experience, so the big question is, Are we able to instill values that they will still be living out ten years from now?

Another thing I wanted to do with the group was to be sure it was not a cloistered group but instead embedded in the world. I want them to learn monastic disciplines but do them in everyday life. So we don't plan to have a monastic softball team. I want to see students engaging the world, identifying a place on our campus where they want to be salt and light. So I tell them that we don't want their lights and lives to revolve around this group, but we want them out there living this radical life, not spending all their time with each other. And it has worked better than I thought it would.

About twenty freshmen come in each year, so by the time we're fully functional I expect there will sixty to a hundred. That many people who are serious about living the Sermon on the Mount really changes the environment.

The group does not live together in one house, though some of the members room together. Religious orders often live together in a monastery or cloister, but we do live in proximity to one another on a campus. One of the reasons for this is that the group is very sensitive about not becoming elitist, self-absorbed, and isolationist. How do you instill values in a group of people in ways that change their lives yet doesn't isolate them so they really make no impact on the world? The trick is not to become isolated but to have a covenant with one another.

The name for the group is Tau Chi Alpha. One of the things it stands for is, "Toughest Christians Alive," and we are quick to say that this is an aspiration not a claim. We refer to ourselves as "Monk Warriors." We want to have the fearlessness of warriors but the discipline of monks. As warriors our weapons are not guns and swords but love and prayer. We're trying to develop skill using weapons that the Spirit of God has given us. So we spend a lot of time talking about prayer and praying. We refer to the dangerous way of prayer—that if you get serious about prayer and open up to God, he's going to mess with you, and do you have the courage to go there?

What do we hope this looks like when these monk warriors leave Abilene? We hope they continue to live out the values in ways appropriate to where they are. They will be radical Jesus where they are. They will combine mission and activity along with the contemplative.

I'm hoping these men will have such a powerful experience of community here that they will try to create these kinds of community where they go—communities of people challenging each other to deeper ways of following Jesus. They also have deep sense of service and mission, that they live not to themselves but for the cause for which Christ died. I want them to have confidence about engaging the world with the lifestyle that they lead. We lead with our lives and the message follows, being salt and light in neighborhoods and churches as well.

I do think it will be much more difficult after this experience to sink into quiet pietism. They will understand that the experience of following Jesus is about a lot more than going to church. I try not to be prescriptive; I want them to identify how to engage in the world, rather than me telling them what it is for each one of them.

The translation is this: It's about living in covenant. I hope they've been inspired to live with others and do life in a different way, sharing with each other a way of life appropriate to their setting—nineteen-year-olds at a Christian university.

The question for us is, What would a life following Christ and living out the Sermon on the Mount look like where we are?

I've told you about the Tau Chi Alpha covenant group because I want to give you a real example of a group of young men who are trying to live out the Sermon on the Mount.

Living the Sermon in Your Community

Now I want to help you form a covenant community step by step . . .

How can I form a covenant community where I live? In other words, how can I form a community of people who agree to live out the Sermon on the Mount?

One question to ask is, Have you decided to live out the sermon yourself? We first live the gospel and the message follows.

If you are reading individually, you might decide to take a spiritual retreat. The forty-day spiritual retreat I took to Lebh Shomea House of Prayer changed my life. Not everyone has the luxury of taking forty days. But we often find ways to do what we really want to do. If you can only go for a few days, you might consider a spiritual retreat or living in the Sermon on the Mount for a certain period of time. For example, you could take the period of Lent to read the Sermon on the Mount daily for those six weeks before Easter. Each day you could read with a different emphasis, using the questions in the chapters in this book, and after a few weeks you could begin committing the Sermon on the Mount to memory.

Now comes the time to approach a friend or fellow follower of Christ. Rather than inviting them into the reading, simply ask for accountability from them. Ask them to hold you accountable to reading and memorizing the Sermon on the Mount. If the friend wants to do it with you, do not stop him or her. But do not urge your friend to do something you have not done yourself. Your friend will be more inspired by you doing it than you urging him or her to do it.

What about in your church? How can you form a group that lives out of the Sermon on the Mount? One very straightforward way that works in most churches is to begin with a "study" of the Sermon on the Mount using this book and the companion film series available on DVD. Begin praying for that study to be more than an attempt to gain greater knowledge but to move toward a greater practice of the teachings of Jesus in the sermon.

Bible classes are a great way to learn and grow spiritually, but most people, even in small groups or Bible classes, never quite form covenant. They never get to the place where they sign on to a covenant agreement with one another to live a certain way.

What if a group could draw up a simple rule and try to live that out? We don't have to be afraid of the word "rule"—it just means a way of life.

In our churches we never quite form covenant. The Church of the Savior in Washington, D.C. has a re-commitment ceremony annually. Each member is asked to agree to a rule of life for the coming year. They agree to hold each other graciously accountable, to live in and out of the gospel. Most churches don't have these covenants, so the Church of the Savior stands out as a great example for us to follow.

For those who want to dig deeper to understand how to form communities outside the monasteries and in churches or other organizations, here are two helpful books:

Christopher Jamison, *Finding Sanctuary: Monastic Steps for Everyday Life*

Dennis Okholm, *Monk Habits for Everyday People: Benedictine Spirituality for Protestants.*

Think of these books, these authors, as mentors leading you as yet another person in your community. I don't think people can do it by themselves; I think they have to find community. See how God shapes it. You don't have to be on campus or in a monastery; you can do it in a church or any situation.

Most of us have a real problem bringing other people into our decision making. Some of us even have trouble bringing God into our decisions. We don't trust others to make the decision that perhaps we've already judged as right or that we want to do. One big problem is that you have to have an active view of the work of the Holy Spirit. We have to have the theology to support this practice. We just don't trust each other to help us make decisions. But in order to trust each other, we have to begin by trusting that God not only works to guide us but also works through others to guide us. God's wisdom gets worked out through the power of the Holy Spirit and in community.

This is easy to say, but we often fall to make decisions alone or alone with God. Have you ever heard someone say, "God told me to do this"? That person may well be listening for God's voice, but often people who say God told me so have trouble listening to the voices of wise counsel that may contradict what God said. And often it seems God is telling them to do exactly what they want to do anyway. So the role of the community is very important. If you believe God is leading you to do something in particular, ask someone you have made a covenant with to help you discern this decision.

One of the big problems small groups face is this: How can we be a covenant group but make room for others in ways that don't adversely affect our group?

Hospitality means welcoming the stranger. You can start in a group by asking for practical ways you can welcome strangers to the group. A friend of mine invited someone to his home group that was in an ongoing conflict with one of the small group members. The relationship needed to be reconciled, but the invitation did not help the situation. The person inviting could have done better to ask the group, "Hey, I'm thinking about inviting this person to our group next week . . . . What do you think?"

A group can also have an open door policy or a closed door policy for certain meetings so you can really get to the business of working on the covenant rule and not always focusing on catching someone up to speed or just hanging out together. This is totally appropriate to have a group time that is just for ones who made a covenant together.

Learning to be hospitable is a lifelong skill you have to cultivate, and when done with a covenant group, it becomes particularly more complex but also more rewarding because you can be hospitable together and have a great impact when someone visits.

Though many of us have a deep desire for community, we often live far from the people with whom we covenant, whether in rural communities or large urban areas. So how do we develop community when we don't have proximity and life is hectic? I believe that choosing a neighborhood to impact is better than living twenty miles from a church and driving from many different directions once a week to meet for a couple of hours. Still, members of churches like that—and there are many in the United States—can ask the question, What neighborhood are we trying to impact? Well, the most obvious would be the one you live in! Covenant groups don't necessarily form around zip codes, but it's much easier to have accountability and interact when you live close.

Proximity is very important. While you may not live together, a campus or a neighborhood is a good geographical boundary for community to thrive. The book, *The New Monastics,* points out that proximity helps planned meetings but also allows for chance encounters along the way. What holds us together are our vows and the commitment to live life in a certain way, but if there aren't opportunities to do that, it is very difficult to hold community together.

What about virtual communities? I'm a little dubious about the potency of virtual communities to do the life change that face-to-face life does. At the same time, I don't want to be a cultural imperialist, as Leonard Sweet calls it, because there may be technological possibilities I'm not familiar with. I don't think you have to live in the same house, but it is good to be close enough for those chance meetings and face-to-face gatherings that are so important. Of course, there's a lot more going on than I know, and it's not like we have to know everything going on with each other.

One of the big issues for churches and groups is that they so deeply want to invite their neighbors, co-workers, friends, and family, but they are afraid they are only inviting them into a one-hour a week community, that there's really not much there outside of a worship service, a class, a few retreats and potlucks a year. What are we really inviting people into when we invite them to church or into a community life? Do we have covenant communities where people can confess their sins, enjoy the grace of Christ and love of neighbors the way God intended? So if the mission is to help people find new community in Christ, is this really a community people can come and participate in with you where you are right now? Or is it something that basically exists one hour a week?

The call of this book is to take the Sermon on the Mount seriously, so it begins with you. When you invite someone in, you certainly ought to be someone living this life so you will be confident of what you are inviting people into.

And we spend our whole lives trying to work out what it means to live according to Jesus' teachings. It begins where we began in this book.

1. You live as a blessed people. Those first beatitudes are not commands; they are blessings. Very difficult to live out when you don't live under or feel the blessing of God.
2. Then you have those six examples about trying to live out a deep inner righteousness, becoming a non-angry, non-lustful, faithful, person of integrity

who does not retaliate, but loves people who don't love you back (your "enemies").
3. Fasting and praying have to do with relationship with God and not putting on a show. We need a different relationship with things.
4. The way we judge or not judge others has to do with generosity toward other people.
5. We often put understanding above doing, but Jesus puts doing it as part of understanding. If I take this seriously, what am I going to have to do differently?

A Sample Rule of Life

The following is the rule used by the Tau Chi Alpha group on the campus of Abilene Christian University

> I commit to live out the Sermon on the Mount as fully as I am able, and to encourage my fellow monk warriors in this way of Life. I affirm the seven basic values of TXA:

Discipline—In a world of whininess and entitlement we inculcate the discipline of monks and the courage and toughness of Jesus. We cultivate physical, mental and spiritual toughness for the sake of our mission. We embrace sacrifice and suffering as qualities of Jesus.

Prayer—We believe transformation in the world and in ourselves begins with learning to pray. We embrace silence, solitude and the contemplative disciplines.

Love—We seek to love indiscriminately as Jesus taught us—love for enemies and "the least of these" especially. We embrace the poor, marginalized and unloved and show respect to every human being as one created in God's image. Hospitality—always being ready to be a welcoming presence—is our way of life.

Mission—We exist for the sake of the cause for which Christ died—the kingdom of God. We live our lives in the world for the sake of the reconciliation and healing of woundedness all around us—we are ministers of Shalom. We embrace the call to leave our comfort zone and be in places of darkness.

Community—We believe God's mission in the world is to create new community, not just change individuals. So we seek to learn to live with our brothers and place their needs over our own. We know we cannot live this life alone.

Joy—We believe this should be fun as we seek the coming-of-the-kingdom every day, and that our joy is not determined by our circumstances. We cultivate thankfulness and hope for the future.

Humility—We are constantly vigilant to ruthlessly rooting out all expressions of religious elitism or superiority in ourselves. We know at our best we are "unprofitable servants."

I make the following vows to God and my brothers.

1. I will read the Sermon on the Mount four times a week and begin to commit it to memory.
2. I will meet for prayer, confession, and encouragement two times a week with another monk warrior.
3. I will treat everyone with respect as ones created in the image and likeness of God. I will value people over technology.
4. In every situation, I will seek to do acts of service, take the lowest place, and place others' needs above my own.
5. I will cultivate the discipline of a warrior. I will do my part to improve our physical benchmarks and excel in school. I will practice the "One"—giving my all. I will not whine.
6. I will cultivate the contemplative life of a monk, by practicing silence, solitude, and fasting. I will enter the dangerous way of prayer. Specifically, I commit to fast one day a week and spend fifteen minutes a day in silence before God.
7. As Jesus taught us, I will be a bearer of love, peace, and reconciliation to those who are Jesus followers and to those who are not—especially to those

who in our world are "the least of these." I will participate in some small way in "the coming of the Kingdom" everyday.

I ask my brothers to hold me graciously accountable to this rule and I pledge to do the same for them, for the sake of the kingdom of God and truly meaningful life.

FURTHER READING

Bessenecker, Scott A. *The New Friars: The Emerging Movement Serving the World's Poor.* Westmont, Ill.: InterVarsity, 2006.

Bonhoeffer, Dietrich. *The Cost of Discipleship.* New York: Simon & Schuster, 1995.

Dobson, Ed. *The Year of Living like Jesus: My Journey of Discovering What Jesus Would Really Do.* Grand Rapids: Zondervan, 2009.

Fleer, David, and Dave Bland, eds. *Preaching the Sermon on the Mount: The World It Imagines.* Atlanta: Chalice, 2007.

Foster, Richard J. *Celebration of Discipline: The Path to Spiritual Growth.* San Francisco: Harper, 1988.

Greenman, Jeffrey P., Timothy Larsen, and Stephen R. Spencer, editors. *The Sermon on the Mount through the Centuries: From the Early Church to John Paul II.* Grand Rapids: Brazos, 2007.

Greig, Pete, and Andy Freeman. *Punk Monk: The New Monasticism and the Ancient Art of Breathing.* Ventura, Calif.: Regal, 2007.

Guelich, Robert A. *The Sermon on the Mount: A Foundation for Understanding.* Waco, Tex.: Word, 1982.

Haase, Albert O.F.M. *Living the Lord's Prayer: The Way of the Disciple.* Westmont, Ill.: InterVarsity, 2009.

Heath, Elaine. *The Mystic Way of Evangelism: A Contemplative Vision for Christian Outreach.* Grand Rapids: Baker, 2008.

Holloway, Gary, and Earl Lavender. *Living God's Love: An Invitation to Christian Spirituality.* Abilene, Tex.: Leafwood, 2004.

Jamison, Christopher. *Finding Sanctuary: Monastic Steps for Everyday Life.* Collegeville, Minn.: Liturgical Press, 2009.

Kendall, R. T. The *Sermon on the Mount: A Verse-by-Verse Look at the Greatest Teachings of Jesus.* Grand Rapids: Chosen Books, 2011.

Okholm, Dennis. *Monk Habits for Everyday People: Benedictine Spirituality for Protestants.* Grand Rapids: Brazos, 2007.

Ortberg, John. *The Life You've Always Wanted: Spiritual Disciplines for Ordinary People.* Grand Rapids: Zondervan, 1997.

Stassen, Glen H. *Living the Sermon on the Mount: A Practical Hope for Grace and Deliverance.* San Francisco: Jossey-Bass, 2006.

Talbert, Charles H. *Reading the Sermon on the Mount: Character Formation and Decision Making in Matthew 5–7.* Grand Rapids: Baker Academic, 2006.

Walker, Jon. *Costly Grace. A Contemporary View of Dietrich Bonhoeffer's* The Cost of Discipleship. Abilene, Tex.: Leafwood, 2010.

Yoder, John Howard. Edited by Glen Stassen, Mark Thiessen Nation, and Matt Hamsher. *The War of the Lamb: The Ethics of Nonviolence and Peacemaking.* Downers Grove, Ill.: InterVarsity, 2009.

Invite **RANDY HARRIS** into Your **SMALL GROUP**

With this 12-episode film series, you can invite Randy Harris into your small group or church class for a challenging encounter with the Sermon on the Mount.

This 2-DVD set provides a guide for group study, personal time, or church viewing for people who want to live the way of Jesus.

- Covers the entire Sermon on the Mount in 12 episodes of 12-15 minutes each (approximately 150 minutes total)
- Designed for use by home groups, church classes, and other groups
- Just the right length to stimulate discussion in a one-hour meeting
- Filmed in High Definition format and suitable for showing on large screens
- Includes original music prepared just for this series
- A challenging and deeply moving call to take the way of Jesus seriously and live it out
- An incredible value—high-quality production values, two DVDs, 150 minutes of content, and an eight-page discussion guide

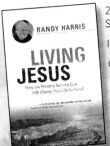

2 DVD set with Study Guide $29.99

ISBN 978-0-89112-370-5

Check out a sample on YouTube

LEAFWOOD
PUBLISHERS
an imprint of Abilene Christian University Press
www.leafwoodpublishers.com
1-877-816-4455 toll free

Also Available

God Work
Confessions of a Standup Theologian

Can theology be practical? Entertaining? Relevant? Anyone who has heard Randy Harris speak will answer with a resounding, "Yes!"

Combining his experience as a professor of theology with a popular style that makes the profound understandable, Harris opens us up to the world as God intends.

"I've seen Randy in front of thousands. No one is better: no one articulates deep, rich, Christ-centered words any better. But I've also witnessed him with one or two students: laughing, praying, encouraging, challenging, befriending. Randy is one of the few people about whom I can say, paraphrasing Paul, 'Follow his example, as he follows the example of Christ.'"

—MIKE COPE,
   Heartbeat Ministries

168 pages $13.99   ISBN 978-0-89112-628-7

an imprint of Abilene Christian University Press
www.leafwoodpublishers.com
1-877-816-4455 toll free

A Companion Volume

Soul Work
Confessions of a Part-Time Monk

Sharing experiences and insights from his visits to monasteries over the years, popular speaker Randy Harris invites us into a richer, fuller life in the Spirit.

Most of us don't have time to visit a monastery for a week or a month. So Randy Harris shows how the monastery can come to you. With wisdom, humor, and captivating insight, he guides you on an unforgettable journey. You will learn prayer, humility, surrender, and quietness along this well-traveled path.

160 pages $13.99   ISBN 978-0-89112-272-2

an imprint of Abilene Christian University Press
www.leafwoodpublishers.com
1-877-816-4455 toll free

Third in the Series

Life Work
Confessions of an Everyday Disciple

In a world gone crazy, what would basic human decency look like?

Are there principles that all humans could follow to make their neighborhoods, countries, and world more just and peaceful? Randy Harris, from his long experience as a teacher of philosophy and ethics, sets out seven basic principles of fair play, justice, and peace.

As a follower of Jesus, Randy, sometimes humorously, always pointedly, focuses on the call of Jesus for a higher righteousness. He places Christian behavior in the context of the cultural contexts of our day, making profound concepts accessible to all his readers.

160 pages $13.99   ISBN 978-0-89112-459-7

an imprint of Abilene Christian University Press
www.leafwoodpublishers.com
1-877-816-4455 toll free